The Methodology (
Empirical Macroecon(

The Methodology of Empirical Macroeconomics stakes out a pragmatic middle ground between traditional, prescriptive economic methodology and recent descriptive (sociological or rhetorical) methodology. The former is sometimes seen as arrogantly telling economists how to do their work and the latter as irrelevant to their practice. The lectures are built around a case study of a concrete example of macroeconomic analysis. They demonstrate that economic methodology and the philosophy of science offer insights that help to resolve the genuine concerns of macroeconomists. Questions addressed include: What is the relationship between theoretical model and empirical observations? What is the relevance of macroeconomics to policy? Should macroeconomics be viewed as a special case of microeconomics? What is the place in macroeconomics of long-standing philosophical issues such as the scope and nature of economic laws, the role of idealizations, methodological individualism, and the problem of causality? Finally, what is an adequate methodology for macroeconomics?

Kevin D. Hoover is Professor and Chair in the Department of Economics at the University of California, Davis. He is the author of *New Classical Macroeconomics: A Sceptical Inquiry* (1988) and *Causality in Macroeconomics* (Cambridge University Press, 2001). Professor Hoover is also the editor of *The Legacy of Robert Lucas* (1999), *Macroeconomics: Development, Tensions, and Prospects* (1995), and the three-volume *New Classical Macroeconomics* (1992), which is in The International Library of Critical Writings in Economics series, and he is the coeditor of *Real-Business-Cycle Models: A Reader* (1998, with J. Hartley and K. Salyer) and of *Monetarism and the Methodology of Economics: Essays in Honour of Thomas Mayer* (1995, with S. Sheffrin). He is a Founding Member and former Chair of the International Network for Economic Method, Vice President of the History of Economics Society, an editor of the *Journal of Economic Methodology*, and an associate editor or on the editorial board of four other journals. Professor Hoover also serves as a research associate at the Federal Reserve Bank of San Francisco and as a lecturer in economics at Balliol College and Lady Margaret Hall, Oxford.

The Methodology of
Empirical Macroeconomics

KEVIN D. HOOVER

University of California, Davis

CAMBRIDGE
UNIVERSITY PRESS

PUBLISHED BY THE PRESS SYNDICATE OF THE UNIVERSITY OF CAMBRIDGE
The Pitt Building, Trumpington Street, Cambridge, United Kingdom

CAMBRIDGE UNIVERSITY PRESS
The Edinburgh Building, Cambridge CB2 2RU, UK
40 West 20th Street, New York, NY 10011-4211, USA
10 Stamford Road, Oakleigh, VIC 3166, Australia
Ruiz de Alarcón 13, 28014 Madrid, Spain
Dock House, The Waterfront, Cape Town 8001, South Africa

http://www.cambridge.org

First published 2001

Printed in the United Kingdom at the University Press, Cambridge

Typeface Times Roman 11/14 pt.   *System* QuarkXPress [BTS]

A catalog record for this book is available from the British Library.

Library of Congress Cataloging in Publication data
Hoover, Kevin D., 1955–
The methodology of empirical macroeconomics / Kevin D. Hoover.
p.   cm.
Includes bibliographical references and index.
ISBN 0-521-80272-5 – ISBN 0-521-00321-0 (pb.)
1. Macroeconomics – Methodology.   I. Title.
HB172.5.H659 2001
339 – dc21   2001018480

ISBN   0 521 80272 5   hardback
ISBN   0 521 00321 0   paperback

We cannot make a science more certain by our wishes or opinions; but we may obviously make it much more uncertain in its application by believing it to be what it is not.

T. Robert Malthus

Contents

Preface

These five lectures were originally delivered in a short course for the Netwerk Algemene en Kwantitatieve Economie (known by the acronym NAKE and rendered into English as the Netherlands Network of Economics). Twice each year the Network, which is a consortium of economics departments of Dutch universities, invites three or four foreign economists to teach students from the various member universities in five-day courses on subjects close to their own research and to consult with graduate students on the students' research. I was privileged to be invited to deliver lectures on methodology at the University of Nijmegen on 8–12 December 1997. This volume is a lightly edited version of those lectures.

These lectures do not aim to be a systematic treatise on methodology. Seven hours of lectures could hardly be that. Instead, they aim to introduce the economically sophisticated student (and I hope the professional economist), who may never have consciously reflected on the methods of the discipline he or she practices, to a few of the most pressing issues of methodology in a single area of economics – empirical macroeconomics. Although these lectures are explicitly concerned with empirical macroeconomics,

Preface

I hope that they nevertheless prove of interest to economists working in other areas as well.

Most economic methodologists divide into two camps. On the one hand, they regard traditional methodology as prescriptive, directing the practice of economists on the basis of philosophical first principles. On the other hand, the recent tendency among methodologists reflects a reaction to the pretensions (arrogance, perhaps) of the methodologist telling the subject-matter specialist how to proceed. The recent approach is more descriptive. It accepts the autonomy of the economic practitioner and tries to understand the internal principles on which he proceeds or, without giving advice, to reconstruct the social or rhetorical strategies that inform his practice. This tendency is often agreeable to economists who wish to dismiss methodology as irrelevant and a waste of time.

In these lectures, however, I explore an alternative, pragmatic approach. The leading notion of this approach is that a relevant methodology must start with the genuine concerns of a particular discipline. Yet careful analysis of those concerns often reveals problems of varying degrees of generality that transcend the concerns and the methods of a single discipline. On this view, methodology and the philosophy of science are not disjoint disciplines from economics, but continuous with it, though operating at a higher level of abstraction. Methodology may sometimes help to solve genuine problems in a particular specialty and is, in that sense, prescriptive.

To remain grounded and relevant, these lectures begin with the consideration of concrete issues in macroeconomics. How should macroeconomic models be formulated? What is the relationship between theoretical models and empirical tests of those models and other empirical observations? What is the relevance of macroeconomic models to policy? Should macroeconomics be viewed as

x

a special case of microeconomics? Questions like these raise issues with a long history in the philosophy of science: the scope and nature of economic laws, the role of idealizations, methodological individualism, and the problem of causality. The first lecture, by way of introduction, considers in detail a particular macroeconomic model and its empirical implementation, highlighting the methodological questions it raises. The second, third, and fourth lectures take a deeper look at some of those problems. The final lecture considers some general methodological questions in light of the previous four lectures.

I am grateful to the Netherlands Network of Economics and especially to its director at the time of my lectures – Professor Ben J. Heijdra, then of the University of Amsterdam (now of the University of Groningen). Professor Heijdra was a warm and generous host, without whom my knowledge of Dutch pub life would have been sadly deficient. The host students of the University of Nijmegen generously devoted their time to providing a pleasant working environment. I am especially grateful to Cornellie van Moorsel and Iman van Leydel, who not only gave up office space for my comfort but also provided me with courteous practical advice on negotiating Nijmegen. I also thank Professors Peter Phillips of Yale University and Ariel Rubinstein of Tel Aviv University, with whom I shared the stage. They were fascinating dinner companions and temporary colleagues. I am grateful to Roger Backhouse and to five anonymous reviewers who read and commented on an earlier draft of these lectures. The lectures have benefited from their many comments. I took the advice with which I agreed – that is, most of it – so long as it was compatible with preserving the shape of the lectures as recognizably those that I had delivered in Nijmegen. Finally, my thanks are due the students in the NAKE course, without whom these lectures would not have been desired or possible. I hope that they got some small proportion of the benefit from hearing the lectures that I derived from writing and delivering them.

I am grateful to John Wiley and Sons for permission to reprint, as Figures 2.1 and 2.2, Figures 8-3 (p. 135) and 38-1 (p. 796) from Robert Resnick and David Halliday, *Physics for Students of Science and Engineering*, copyright © 1960, John Wiley and Sons, New York.

1

Some Methodological
Problems in Macroeconomics

Some Methodological Problems in Macroeconomics

A PHILOSOPHER IS TRANSFORMED INTO AN ECONOMIST

I began my academic career at the College of William and Mary in Virginia. I studied philosophy and was particularly interested in the philosophy of science. As is common in many American universities, I lived in college housing and had a roommate, who, as it happens, studied economics and is now also an economics professor. He used to tell me stories about how economists thought about the world, and I used to laugh and tell him how absurd economists must be. The story that sticks in my mind is the one in which businesses such as ice cream vendors on a beach (monopolistic competitors) are thought of as points distributed at regular intervals on a circle. Pretty silly – at least to one who had never thought for five minutes about competition. After taking my degree, I won a scholarship that allowed me to study at Balliol College, Oxford; and, more or less accidentally, I began to study economics and became hooked. But I came to economics with a philosopher's sensibility.

After taking another bachelor's degree at Oxford, I returned to the States and worked for the Federal Reserve Bank of San Francisco. Here the economics was entirely concerned with practical issues in monetary policy and macroeconomics. This was not long after Christopher Sims had popularized the use of Granger-causality tests in monetary economics.[1] I recall my utter amazement at the power of econometrics to reduce a fraught question such as the nature of causality to a relatively simple test. But at

[1] Sims (1972).

3

Oxford I had been reared a Keynesian, and at the Fed, the Granger-causality tests were supporting monetarism. So for not very admirable reasons I began to wonder about the soundness of these tests. I began to think about them philosophically.

But economists, on the whole, do not have much use for philosophy; and, even when they do, not for the sort of philosophy that interested me. This was illustrated for me when, after a couple of years, I returned to Oxford to work on a doctorate. Amartya Sen, an economist with well-known philosophical interests, had some formal administrative responsibility for me – the sort that required only one meeting to obtain a signature. I went to see him at All Souls College, and he welcomed me, offered me a sherry, and asked some questions as a prelude to giving me his signature. At some point, he expressed bafflement that I professed to be interested in philosophy and yet was not particularly interested in the nature of rationality or in economic justice – the kind of philosophy that captured his attention. Perhaps, in a great tradition that goes back to Adam Smith and even earlier, Sen sees economics as a moral discipline rather than as a science analogous to physics or chemistry. In contrast, at the Federal Reserve I had seen policy makers trying to get a true understanding of what the economy was actually like as a guide to policy actions. And even if those policy actions were grounded in moral concerns, the scientific question, what is the economy like?, seemed to be logically prior. In my doctoral dissertation I tried to connect monetary theory with philosophical concerns to answer the question that worried the Federal Reserve: does money cause prices?

4

I have always regarded myself – even as I have written more and more on methodology – as principally a monetary economist or macroeconomist. My interests in philosophy of science and methodology have always been grounded in the detailed practice of macroeconomics.

Is there a difference between methodology and the philosophy of science? I was asked that question by a philosopher at a conference and, despite the fact that I am an editor of the *Journal of Economic Methodology* and should have had an answer, I never have found myself satisfied with any answer that I have either given or entertained. I will not try to draw that distinction here. Nevertheless, since it is a part of my title, I should, perhaps, at least consider some definitions of "methodology." The first is due to Mark Blaug, an economist: methodology is

> a study of the relationship between theoretical concepts and warranted conclusions about the real world; in particular, methodology is that branch of economics where we examine the ways in which economists justify their theories and the reasons they offer for preferring one theory over another; methodology is both a descriptive discipline – "this *is* what most economists do" – and a prescriptive one – "this is what economists *should* do to advance economics."[2]

Alexander Rosenberg, a philosopher, offers a different definition: a methodology is a set of rules generated by

[2] Blaug (1992), p. xii.

particular theories.[3] Formally, the rules, R, are a function of the theory, t. As theories develop, t' replaces t, and the methodology changes: $R(t') \neq R(t)$.

These two definitions are different but not contradictory. Rosenberg's definition is one in which the changing fine details of particular theories and practices are central to the methodology itself, while Blaug's is more global and overarching. And while there is a certain irony in the fact that it is not the economist but the philosopher for whom the details of particular theories are defining, there is no reason not to view the definitions as complementary: Rosenberg's methodologies are the objects that Blaug's methodology studies. We might refer to Rosenberg's interests as *methodological* and to Blaug's as *metamethodological*. Most of these lectures shall focus on – or at least begin with – methodological questions in Rosenberg's sense. It is only in the final lecture that we return to metamethodological issues in Blaug's sense.

I will also adopt another position from Rosenberg, which I will not explicitly defend, but hope to illustrate in these lectures. This is what I have elsewhere called Rosenberg's *continuity thesis*: there are no defined boundaries between economics as practiced by economists, methodology of economics, philosophy of science as applied to economics, and philosophy of science.[4] Each discipline blends seamlessly into the other; and the conclusions of each discipline, while they may have different degrees of relevance for the practice of economics, have relevance of the same kind.

---

[3] Rosenberg (1992), p. 10.   [4] Hoover (1995), p. 720.

Some Methodological Problems in Macroeconomics

It would help to have an example of macroeconomics to work with. For several reasons I choose Christopher Pissarides's paper "Loss of Skill during Unemployment and the Persistence of Employment Shocks."[5] First, this paper is a good example of state-of-the-art macroeconomics, illustrating a number of features that are now considered by the mainstream of the profession to be essential – particularly, an approach that starts with optimization in a microfoundational framework. It is chosen not because it of its individual importance – excellent paper though it is. Rather, it is chosen as a *typical* example of a genre for which any number of other examples might have served just as well. Second, although the paper does not present empirical results, it is concerned with a genuine empirical policy issue (namely, the persistence of unemployment) and considers the implications of its theoretical analysis for the behavior of data. Third, the paper has already received specific attention from Nancy Cartwright, a philosopher of science, whose views we will examine in Chapter 2.

Pissarides begins with the observation that macroeconomic aggregates are persistent; that is, deviations of the aggregates from their trends are serially correlated. In particular, he wants to understand why shocks to employment persist for long periods. On the basis of previously known empirical evidence, he hypothesizes that unemployed workers lose skills the longer they are unemployed. He suggests that this could produce a thin-market externality

---

[5] Pissarides (1992).

7

even if employers could not discriminate between the long-term and short-term unemployed in hiring. The general idea is that a firm supplies jobs and has a random chance of being matched to employees. A negative shock to unemployment lowers the average skill level of the pool of available workers. Since the firm's expected profit from supplying a job is lower when the skill level is lower, the firm offers fewer jobs. But in offering fewer jobs, the firm insures that those who are not hired will lose skills, so that the pool remains thin or de-skilled not only long after the shock but even if all the original laid-off workers are no longer in the pool. Unemployment is persistent.

Now, the idea of Pissarides's paper is simple and plausible. The paper itself is aimed at formalizing the idea and, in turn, deriving implications from the formal model. Pissarides gives us an overlapping-generations model with equal cohorts of identical agents who live for two periods. The unemployed produce no output. The young employed and those old employed who were also employed while young produce one unit of output. The old employed who were unemployed when young produce less than a unit of output.

Workers and firms are matched randomly each period. They must agree either to cooperate in production for the period or to forgo production. A firm matched to a previously unemployed worker cannot reject that worker to search for a higher-productivity worker in the same period. Workers and firms enter into a Nash bargain, splitting the marginal return to the worker's production equally between them. Pissarides makes assumptions that avoid corner solutions, so that employment depends upon the intensity of the firms' search for workers – that is, on the number of jobs supplied. A firm chooses its job supply conditional on the expected skill level of the employees – that is, on the mix of short-term and long-term unemployed in the labor force. Since last period's job supply determines this period's long-term unemployment, the skill level is itself a dynamic characteristic. In general, unemployment is persistent.

Even in such a simple model, the details are hard to analyze in general, but for quite particular forms of a firm's search function, it is possible to show that some choices of parameters can generate multiple equilibria of a form such that favorable shocks generate long periods of full employment and unfavorable shocks long periods of unemployment. The model could be extended to permit firms to discriminate against the de-skilled workers. In fact, since that extension does not change the qualitative conclusions, Pissarides actually extends it by making the intensity of each worker's search depend on the duration of the worker's unemployment. The result is a discouraged-worker effect that implies serial correlation in the average duration of unemployment as well as in aggregate unemployment.

The first form of Pissarides's model results in two key equations:[6]

$$J_t = Lk[1 + y + (1 - y)q_{t-1}]q_t, \qquad (1.1)$$

where J is the number of jobs, L is the number of workers in each generation, k is the inverse of the cost of opening

---

[6] Equations (1.1) and (1.2) correspond to Pissarides's (1992, pp. 1376–77) equations (7) and (8).

a job for one period, y is a productivity parameter, q is the probability of a match between a job seeker and a job opening, and subscripts indicate the relevant time; and

$$q_t = \min\{x(J_t/2L, 1), 1\}, \qquad (1.2)$$

where $x(.\,,.)$ is a twice-differentiable function with positive first-order and negative second-order derivatives, homogeneous of degree 1 and satisfying[7]

$$x(0, 2L) = x(J_t, 0) = 0 \qquad (1.3)$$

and

$$x(J_t, 2L) \leq \max\{J_t, 2L\}. \qquad (1.4)$$

Equations (1.1) and (1.2) together simultaneously determine the number of jobs offered and the probability of a job match.

Pissarides relates his model to real-world data in the following way. He asks us to consider two general empirical equations:[8]

$$v = F(\phi, w, s, d) \qquad (1.5)$$

and

$$q = G(v, s, c, \sigma), \qquad (1.6)$$

[7] Equations (1.3) and (1.4) correspond to Pissarides's (1992, p. 1375) equations (2) and (3).
[8] Equations (1.5) and (1.6) correspond to Pissarides's (1992, p. 1387) equations (31) and (32).

where v is the measure of vacant jobs, ϕ and w "are the usual variables that influence the demand for labor in frictionless models," s is the number of job seekers, d is the duration structure of unemployment, c is the intensity of search, and σ is a measure of mismatch or sectoral shifts. The left-hand variable of equation (1.6), q, is the matching rate, a flow variable. Empirically, we might want to replace q with the employment rate, which is its stock equivalent, or with the unemployment rate. In the latter case, equations (1.5) and (1.6) together imply the dynamics of the Beveridge curve – the contemporaneous relationship between the vacancy rate and the unemployment rate.

Equations (1.1) and (1.2) refer to variables defined within the confines of the model itself. The variables in (1.5) and (1.6) largely have different names from the variables in (1.1) and (1.2) and refer (generically at least) to real-world aggregate time-series data. There is a correspondence between the two sets of variables. Roughly, v in equation (1.5) corresponds to J in equation (1.1). The variables ϕ and w are parameters in the theoretical model ($\phi = 2$ and $w = 1$) and so do not show up explicitly. The variable d is a summary measure reflecting the time dependence induced by the interaction of the two matching probabilities at different dates, q_{t-1} and q_t. In equation (1.2), s corresponds to L, and c "is implicit in"

$$S_t = q_t\left[1 + y + q_{t-1}^2(1 - y)\right]L. \qquad (1.7)$$

"[S]ectoral shifts [σ] were ignored in the theoretical discussion."[9]

---

[9] Equation (1.7) corresponds to Pissarides's (1992, p. 1382) equation (19).

The Methodology of Empirical Macroeconomics

In discussing the two empirical equations and their relationship to the model, Pissarides notes that in the extended model, in which search intensity is endogenous, the falling search intensity after a negative shock slows down the recovery of the matching rate relative to the vacancy rate, and that this is a feature of the data as it corresponds to counterclockwise loops in vacancy/unemployment space.

SOME METHODOLOGICAL ISSUES

Pissarides's paper is interesting in its own right and suggests many avenues of further research. It is also representative of a number of very general methodological issues. Let us consider a list that is by no means exhaustive but corresponds roughly to the topics that I shall take up in subsequent lectures. The overarching theme is, how do theoretical macroeconomic models such as Pissarides's model relate to empirical data?

Pissarides cites the qualitative dynamic behavior of vacancies and unemployment (the counterclockwise loops) as a plus for his model because analogous variables in it show a similar pattern. In the argot of macroeconomics: the model accounts for the *stylized facts*. So,

> 1 *What in general is the relationship between rough-and-ready empirical generalizations (the stylized facts) and models that appear to imply them?*

Pissarides's model analyzes the behavior of individual agents. Again, to use the common jargon, it is a *micro-*

12

foundational model. But the assumptions that it makes about economic agents are wildly unrealistic: for example, the overlapping-generations model with identical agents who live for two periods, randomized job search for both workers and firms, absence of discrimination against long-term unemployed workers. What is more, the aggregation is a matter of simply summing up the behavior of individual agents. The clear intent of many such models, despite the *unrealisticness*, is to connect to measured empirical data.[10] This raises at least three questions:

2 *What is the correspondence between the variables in the theory and the qualitatively distinct variables that are empirically observed?*

3 *What quantitative implications does a model known to be unrealistic in some dimensions have for measured economic data?*

4 *How can one judge the quantitative success of an unrealistic model?*

Pissarides's model is a sort of representative-agent model. The term *representative-agent model* is often restricted to those models in which the behavior of a single infinitely lived optimizing agent represents the macroeconomic behavior of the aggregate of consumer/workers or firms or both. In this sense, an overlap-

---

[10] "Unrealisticness" is the negative of "realisticness," an ugly neologism coined by Uskali Mäki (1996). Despite its lack of grace or charm, "realisticness" is useful when, as Mäki suggests, it is distinguished from "realism": the first has to do with accuracy of representation, the second with whether or not the things represented exist independently.

ping-generations model is not a representative-agent model, because it involves an infinite number of agents. I call it a representative-agent model, however, because all agents are reduced to a few representative types. In this case there are two types: firms and workers. The workers are all identical, albeit in any period some are young and some are old. The young will become exactly like the old in the next period; the old were exactly like the young the period before. Aggregation – the process of connecting the microeconomic to the macroeconomic – proceeds in one of two ways in representative-agent economies. With representative-agent models taken strictly, aggregation is by analogy: an individual optimization problem is simply blown up to the size of the entire economy. With an overlapping-generations model, as here, aggregation is by simple summation: we add up the individual behaviors because each agent is like the other. Now, this raises an important question:

5 *Is either aggregation strategy an adequate microfoundation for macroeconomics?*

But there is an even more basic question in the wings:

6 *Are microfoundations for macroeconomics essential or even posssible?*

Pissarides's model has no direct linkage to economic policy. Yet, one could easily imagine extensions of it that permit policy to play a role. The current model might, with or without such an extension, convey useful information to a policy maker. As soon as we begin to talk about policy controlling the economy, we raise issues of causality. At least two questions arise immediately:

7 *In what sense can a macroeconomic model be regarded as causal, and how can its causal structure be related to policy?*

8 *How can we assess whether the causal structure implicit in a macroeconomic model corresponds to the causal structure of the world itself?*

Pissarides's model (or any other competent macroeconomic model) will, no doubt, raise many other methodological questions. But these are suggestive of the questions that I wish to address in the next three lectures. I have more strongly held views on some of these questions than on others. And I do not believe that any of these questions can be definitively resolved in the course of these lectures. I shall be content if I can convince the reader that these are important questions and that considerations beyond those found in economics narrowly construed are relevant to their answers.

SUGGESTED READINGS

The best general introduction to the methodology of economics is Mark Blaug's *The Methodology of Economics: Or How Economists Explain*, 2nd ed. (Cambridge: Cambridge University Press, 1992). While there were many books written on the methodology of economics, going back to the nineteenth century, the professionalization of methodology in economics can be dated from the first edition of Blaug's book in 1980.

Blaug is an economist who has read and thought about philosophy but who remains principally concerned with what economists do. In contrast, Daniel Hausman is a philosopher who has thought about economics but is mainly concerned with a detached understanding of economics as a philosophical problem. The "Appendix" of Hausman's *The Inexact and Separate Science of Economics* (Cambridge: Cambridge University Press, 1992) is an excellent bridge between the methodology of economics and the philosophy of science and a compact summary of the philosophy of science with economists as the target readers. The main text, which focuses on microeconomics and argues for a controversial understanding of the nature of economics, is also worth reading.

For those who want to know more about the philosophy of science, Ian Hacking's *Representing and Intervening* (Cambridge: Cambridge University Press, 1983) is a fine starting point. Beautifully and engagingly written, it is intended as an introductory text for undergraduates; yet, as befits a first-rate philosopher, Hacking does not hesitate to make arguments of which other professional philosophers must take notice.

Of course, Christopher Pissarides's article, "Loss of Skill during Unemployment and the Persistence of Employment Shocks," *Quarterly Journal of Economics* 107(4) (1992), 1371–91, is the foil for the three core lectures of this book. As I observe in this lecture, notwithstanding that many other papers could have served the same function, it is an excellent paper in its own right and well worth study.

2

Are There
Macroeconomic Laws?

We begin with Pissarides's model, which I described in the first lecture. What is his purpose in offering that model? One presumes that it is to explain the facts. But oddly only one empirical fact is mentioned in the paper – namely, that unemployment and vacancies arrange themselves in counterclockwise loops when plotted against one another. Nevertheless, Pissarides proposes to test his model by estimating versions of equations (1.5) and (1.6) and checking to see that the quantitative and qualitative implications of the model actually hold in the data. The model would then be regarded as an explanation of its true implications. The fact that the model makes no reference to the particularities of any place or time, but only broadly and implicitly to a market-based economy, suggests that he would generalize and claim that the success of his model on one set of data (one country, one sample period) justifies using it as a generic explanation of other similar sets of data, although one could always challenge its relevance by testing it directly on the similar data sets. This is, I think, a fairly common understanding among economists of the purposes of models. The methodological question that it raises is this: *what is the explanatory relationship between a macroeconomic model and empirical observations?*

A STANDARD VIEW

It is much easier to make a persuasive case for a view if one has another plausible view that it can refute. Rhetorically, we credit the knight more for slaying the dragon than for his own special virtues. The usual dragon, the most common foil, in discussions of scientific explanation is the *covering-law model of explanation*. This view has its roots in the work of John Stuart Mill, who was an important economist as well as a philosopher and a logician.[1]

A standard definition of a *scientific law* is a true, universal generalization. This view is clear in the works of David Hume, another economist-philosopher.[2] It is not a complete definition as it stands. It may be a true, universal generalization that everyone attending the 10 A.M. NAKE lecture on 9 December 1997 was born after 1945; but it is not a law. It is less clear, however, that the proposition that everyone attending the lecture was born after 1945 is not a law. What is wrong with the first generalization is that one is not willing to infer from its truth that by virtue of the law the next person to enter the lecture hall must have been born after 1945.[3] Clearly, if one of our fathers or grandfathers were that next person, there is nothing about the lecture hall that would alter the facts of his birth. The ambiguity of the second generalization comes about because we do not believe that there would be any possibility whatsoever of someone more than one thousand years old entering the lecture hall.

Still, how to flesh out the idea that this is so by virtue of the supposed law is problematic. One approach offered by philosophers is to say that we can call a proposition a law only if there are true *counterfactual* or *subjunctive* state-

---

[1] Mill (1851). [2] Hume (1739, 1742, 1777).

[3] Some would also object that the references to specific times and places in these examples undermine the universality of their claims and so disqualify them as laws. That is debatable, but it is not the point at issue here.

ments that back it up. We reject the law because it is not true "that if a person had entered the lecture hall, he would necessarily have been born after 1945" or "that if a person were to enter the lecture hall, he would necessarily be born after 1945." But this does not get us too far; for when one asks what determines the truth of counterfactuals or subjunctives, a popular philosophical response says that they are true just when there is a law that makes their consequent follow from their antecedent. We argue in a circle.

Now these puzzles are the tip of a large philosophical iceberg that may threaten the very idea of a scientific law. But I would like to set them to one side and simply treat laws as true, universal generalizations subject to the caveat that we mean nonaccidental generalizations (that is, generalizations not like the one about the ages of the people in the lecture hall) and that we know what those are when we see them.

A typical covering-law explanation is an answer to a question such as, why is this steel ball falling at ninety-eight meters per second? The form of the explanation is

$Velocity = (9.8m/s^2) \times time$ — The covering law

The ball was dropped 10 seconds ago and has not yet hit the ground. — Initial conditions

(The covering law and Initial conditions together form the) Explanans

The ball is falling at 98 m/s. — Conclusion — Explanandum

21

This sort of covering-law explanation is also known as a *deductive-nomological* explanation because the *explanandum* follows deductively from one or more major premises, the *covering laws* (hence "nomological" from the Greek *nomos* = law), and one or more minor premises, the *initial conditions*. Together they form the *explanans*.

Laws may be related hierarchically. The law

$$V = gt,$$

in which V is velocity, g is the constant of gravitational acceleration, and t is time, is explained by Newton's theory of kinetics, which gives one law:

$$F = ma,$$

in which F is force, m is mass, and a is acceleration; and by Newton's law of universal gravitation, which gives another law:

$$F = GmM/R^2,$$

in which m and M are two masses, R is the distance between them, and $G = 6.67 \times 10^{-11}$ newtons-m^2/kg^2 is the universal gravitational constant; and by initial conditions:

$M = M_e$, the mass of the earth

$R = R_e$, the distance between m and the center of the earth.

Together these imply

$$a = GM_e/R_e \equiv g$$

from which

$$V = gt$$

follows immediately.

The power of deductive-nomological explanations is felt most keenly when the explanations unwind complexities. Consider a sheet of paper and a steel ball dropped from fifteen thousand meters. Despite the universal law of gravitation, the following are empirical facts:

a. The two objects accelerate at different rates.
b. Neither object continues to accelerate; rather, each reaches (a different) terminal velocity [a lucky thing too; otherwise parachutes would not work].

The covering-law model explains these facts by an appeal to a second law, which states that wind resistance (a force operating in the opposing direction to gravity) is directly proportional to the ratio of surface area to mass and directly proportional to velocity. Thus, when the velocity of any object reaches a point such that the wind resistance is equal and opposite to the force of gravity, the object ceases to accelerate. This happens at a lower velocity for a sheet of paper (high area to mass ratio) than for a steel ball (low area to mass ratio).

There is great beauty in such covering-law explanations when they work. But they do not always work. That the acceleration due to gravity is independent of the mass of the objects is borne out to a high degree of accuracy in

Galileo's experiments with balls dropped along inclined planes (and, in the apocryphal version, with balls dropped from the Leaning Tower of Pisa) and to an even higher degree of accuracy with balls dropped by astronauts on the Moon. But these are not typical cases. Otto Neurath gives the example of predicting the path of a banknote being blown through St. Stephen's Square in Vienna.[4] With all the measuring equipment in the world and the most powerful computers, prediction of the exact path of the banknote based on Newton's laws and initial conditions is not possible. There will always be some error. We cannot always use the covering-law account to unwind the complexity of observed phenomena.

One strategy is to say that the laws are completely universal and that, if we only had enough computing power and detailed enough initial conditions, we could calculate the path of the banknote. Lacking these prerequisites, we may nevertheless say that the laws hold ceteris paribus. But here, as with a banknote whose convertibility has been suspended, the ceteris paribus condition is a promise to pay in the future that will never be redeemed. Some hard phenomena may be tameable if we lower our sights and seek, not a deductive-nomological explanation, but what covering-law theorists call an *inductive-statistical explanation*. In this case, the laws hold only probabilistically, and the inferences are not to what happens, but to the probability that it happens. While this looks rather more like what we face in economics, we should notice that not every phenomenon will succumb to an inductive-statistical

---

[4] Neurath's example is cited by Cartwright (1994), p. 283.

explanation without the promissory note of unredeemable ceteris paribus clauses.

Are there universal empirical generalizations in economics? Well, there are lots of things that economists call laws:

- the law of demand
- Engel's law
- Okun's law
- Gresham's law
- the law of one price
- the law of diminishing returns
- Walras's law
- Say's law
- and perhaps some that I have missed.

These economic laws are a hodge-podge. Some are axioms, some analytical truths, some heuristic rules. But at least the first four are robust empirical generalizations of a very imprecise form. The law of demand, for example, states that when the price of a good rises, demand for that good falls. The law does not say how much demand falls for any given increase in price. And we know that there are (relatively rarely) exceptions to the law, which we may believe that we can explain as deductions from an enlarged set of theoretical premises in the same way that we can explain why paper has a lower terminal velocity

25

than a steel ball (the Giffen good provides a textbook example).

What we need to ask, however, is whether macroeconomic models such as Pissarides's model really trade in such robust empirical generalizations and their higher-level precursors. One might interpret equations (1.5) and (1.6) as laws. But this, I think, turns matters upside down. The fact that Pissarides presents these equations without having estimated them shows that they are not themselves robust empirical generalizations that theory is to explain. Rather they, or at least some aspects of them (the variables and the expected signs of their corresponding coefficients, for instance), are implications of the theory. When they are eventually estimated, if they prove not to be consonant with the theory or not to be robust, it would lead us to reconsider the details of the model. These empirical equations are not laws. They are instead observational structures with few qualitative and no quantitative implications. They are forms that have to be filled in econometrically.

More than that, the linkage between these equations and the model is exceedingly loose. The conceptual description of the theoretical data does not match very tightly the description of the actual observable data that will be used to estimate the equations. The relationship between the model and the empirical equations, even after they are estimated, is analogical. It requires an imaginative leap to draw conclusions about the model from the empirical equations or about the equations from the model.

Compare the situation just described with respect to a typical macroeconomic model to the situation described in the illustrations of the covering-law account of falling objects. One is inclined to conclude that economics does not look much like a physical science. Or does it? It sur-prising to those of us brought up on the image of physics as the model of scientific certainty and scope that a number of philosophers of science have begun to argue that physics is more like economics than it is like its popular image.[5] Their point is that even so compelling an explanatory account as that of the falling balls is not so simple, and that we think that it is simple mainly because we learned it from textbooks rather than from dropping balls from airplanes. To get a steel ball to behave in fairly strict accordance with the law of gravity, we need not only to account for wind resistance but also to shield it from turbulence, to account for humidity and temperature changes, and so forth. In other words, it is not enough just

---

[5] A glib objection to this image of physics would be to say that quantum mechanics with the Heisenberg uncertainty principle and probabil-ities brought in at the ground floor should have already rendered the image obsolete. But this would be radically to misunderstand the claims of quantum mechanics. Even though it stands on an indeter-ministic basis, quantum electrodynamics is one of the most precise theories known to science. Richard Feynman (1985, p. 7) gives one of several possible examples: experiments have determined Dirac's number to be 1.00115965221 (with an uncertainty of about 4 in the last digit), while theory predicts that it is 1.00115965246 (with uncer-tainty about 5 times greater than the experimental measurement – that is, about 2 in the next-to-last digit). Feynman writes: "To give you some feeling for the accuracy of these numbers, it comes out some-thing like this: If you were to measure the distance from Los Angeles to New York to this accuracy, it would be exact to the thickness of a human hair . . . By the way, I have chosen only one number . . . [t]here are other things in quantum electrodynamics that have been mea-sured with comparable accuracy, which also agree very well . . . These numbers are meant to intimidate you into believing that the theory is probably not too far off!"

to say the law of gravity holds ceteris paribus; if we are going to see the law of gravity in action, we must in practice fulfill substantial parts of those ceteris paribus conditions (or account for what happens when we do not). Only in a rare set of instances can this be done reliably and effectively. How things will behave when we do not cash out the ceteris paribus conditions is anybody's guess. The falling steel ball exemplifies, at best, a small subset of physical phenomena. Most phenomena are more like Neurath's banknote blowing through St. Stephen's Square. Nancy Cartwright puts this point well. Of the laws of physics, she writes:

> It is hard to find them in nature and we are always having to make excuses for them: why they have exceptions – big or little; why they only work for models in the head; why it takes an engineer with a special knowledge of materials and a not too literal mind to apply physics to reality.[6]

NOMOLOGICAL MACHINES

Cartwright proposes that we replace the idea of scientific laws as universal generalizations with one in which laws emerge only in quite specific circumstances. Empirical regularities on this view are not robust but highly special. Physical sciences focus on the controlled experiment

[6] Cartwright (1989), p. 8.

precisely because controlled experiments are what make empirical regularities appear robustly. It is only in the context of the right apparatus that the law is evident. Saying that a law holds ceteris paribus is too cheap unless we say just which other things have to be held equal for the law to appear. But when we cash out the ceteris paribus clauses, we must be careful how we generalize the scope of the law. The claim of universality is a never warranted leap of faith.

Cartwright takes experiments seriously and metaphorically. Laws as robust empirical regularities in limited domains are explained as the output of *nomological machines* (that is, machines that make laws). Scientific models are thought of as blueprints for nomological machines. Anyone who has ever built anything, following a blueprint or not, knows that machines have parts and parts have properties in virtue of which the machines function. While Cartwright wants to nix our habit of generalizing the empirical regularities outside the context of the nomological machines that produce them, she is willing to generalize some of the properties of the parts. The various parts of the machine have *capacities* – that is, enduring properties carried between contexts but not necessarily realized in every context. Aspirin, for example, has the capacity to cure headaches – it sometimes is effective in doing so, but there are contexts in which it fails to do so as well. Parts have capacities, and assemblages of parts also have capacities – different from, but related to those of the parts. The capacity of an old-fashioned clock to tell time emerges from the properties of gears to translate the direction of rotational motion and of springs to store kinetic energy.

The gear or the spring carries its capacities into other contexts (for example, into a wind-up or "clockwork" toy), and
it retains its capacity even when it is not exhibiting it (the
toy sits unloved on the shelf or the gear is in the clock-
maker's bin of replacement parts). Different things may
carry the same capacity. A rubber fan belt or a woman's
nylon stocking suitably twisted and tied both have the
capacity to turn the alternator in automobile. The best
interpretation of Newton's "law" of universal gravitation
on this view is perhaps as a capacity shared by anything
with a mass.

There are many standard examples in physics that can be
regarded as nomological machines. Consider one, a harmonic oscillator. Figure 2.1 illustrates such an oscillator, the
parts of which are a mass and a spring. The relevant capacity of the spring is described by Hooke's law: the force of
an elastic material is opposite the direction of deformation
and proportional to the size of the deformation. And the
capacities of the mass are described by Newton's first law
(inertia) and second law ($F = ma$). The capacity of the
whole machine is to exhibit oscillatory motion. The capacity to oscillate is also exhibited electrically by an LC circuit
consisting of a coil and a capacitor (see Figure 2.2). The
analogy with the spring and mass is exact.[7] Both harmonic
oscillators are described by a common dynamic equation:

$$A\frac{d^2z}{dt^2} + Bz = 0.$$

The correspondences are shown in Table 2.1.

---

[7] Resnick and Halliday (1960), p. 797.

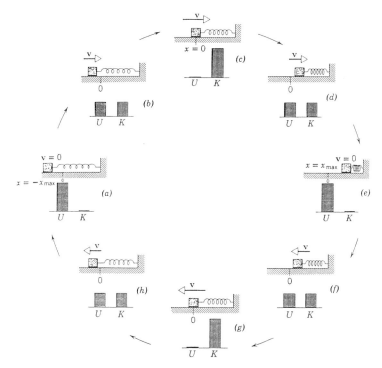

Figure 2.1. A mass-and-spring harmonic oscillator. A mass
attached to a spring slides back and forth on a frictionless
surface. The system is called a harmonic oscillator. The motion
of the mass through one cycle is illustrated. Starting at the
left (9 o'clock) the mass is in its extreme left position and
momentarily at rest: $K = 0$. The spring is extended to its
maximum length: $U = U_{max}$. (K and U are illustrated in the
bar graphs below each sketch.) An eighth-cycle later (next
drawing) the mass has gained kinetic energy, but the spring is
no longer so elongated; K and U have here the same value,
$K = U = U_{max}/2$. At the top the spring is neither elongated nor
compressed and the speed is at a maximum: $U = 0$, $K = K_{max} =$
U_{max}. The cycle continues, with the total energy $E = K + U$
always the same: $E = K_{max} = U_{max}$. *Source*: Resnick and
Halliday (1960), Figure 8-3, p. 135.

31

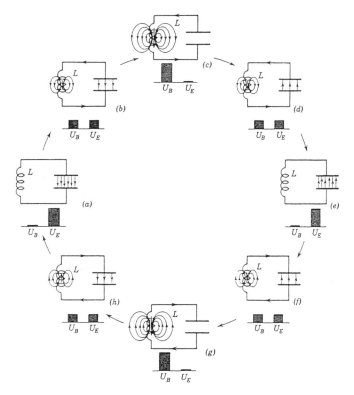

Figure 2.2. An inductance-capacitance (*LC*) harmonic oscillator, showing various stages in the oscillation of an *LC* circuit. The bar graphs below each figure show the stored magnetic and electric potential energy. The vertical arrows on the inductor axis show the current. The student should compare this figure in detail to Figure 2.1, to which it exactly corresponds. *Source*: Resnick and Halliday (1960), Figure 38-1, p. 796.

Table 2.1. *Correspondences between two harmonic oscillators governed by* $A\dfrac{d^2 z}{dt^2} + Bz = 0$

	Interpretation	
Coefficient	Mass-and-spring oscillator	Inductance-capacitance oscillator
A	mass	inductance
B	distance	(inverse) capacitance
z	force	charge

IDEALIZATION AND ANALOGY

The view that science is about the construction of nomological machines and the identification of the capacities that govern their functioning highlights the fact that it often requires great cleverness to generate robust empirical regularities. They often appear only in situations in which they are shielded from confounding influences and in which the domain is restricted (for example, only dense objects with low surface areas falling for brief times conform closely to the law of gravity). This view has plausibility in physical sciences, but does it apply to macroeconomics? Are there nomological machines in macroeconomics? And are macroeconomic models blueprints for nomological machines?

These are different questions. But Cartwright answers "yes" to both of them. However, I do not think that a comparison of the physical examples already seen and Pissarides's model supports Cartwright's affirmative response to the second question – that is, that Pissarides's model is a blueprint for the nomological machine.

If I wish to build a harmonic oscillator, Figures 2.1 and 2.2 tell me how to do it. I can buy a spring and a weight or a capacitor and a coil and assemble them as in the diagrams – and they will in fact oscillate. I will have some trouble getting a frictionless plane; but there are well-known tactics (oil, bearings, etc.) for reducing friction so that my apparatus will conform closely, albeit not perfectly, to the textbook description of the model. But where do I go to find identical people with two-period lives or markets that operate by random matching? Not only are these assumptions special – as indeed they are in the physical examples – but they have only a weak correspondence to the actual world. I can use Pissarides's model as a blueprint, but as a blueprint for another model (for example, a computer simulation), not as a blueprint for an actual economy.

One response to this criticism is to say that Pissarides's model is an analogy or a metaphor. Yes, the correspondence of the model, part by part, is weak; but, taken as a whole, the model gives an image of the qualitative performance of the economy that can be checked through empirical work. There is, I think, a lot in this response, and it gives a reasonable interpretation of the gap between Pissarides's theoretical summary equations, (1.1), (1.2), and (1.7), and his proposed empirical equations, (1.5) and (1.6). Nevertheless, it leaves open the question of how this model relates to rival explanatory models and how both, in turn, relate to empirical data. How do data confirm or disconfirm models that are only analogically related to them? And how do data help to discriminate among rival explanatory models?

An alternative account of the relationship between the model and the world is given in the notion that a successful model is an *idealization* of the world. This account is developed in detail by Leszek Nowak, using the example of Marxist economics – though he means it to apply quite generally to all science.[8] Nowak's idea is that the behavior of things in the economy or in the world is the result of complicated interactions of numerous *primary* and *secondary* factors. An idealized model isolates the characteristics of the primary factors by setting the secondary factors to extreme values (zero or infinity) at which point their influence can be neglected. That is, if, in the world, the secondary factors really were at their extreme values, then the world really would behave as the primary factors in the model say it will. So, in our example of deriving $V = gt$ from the gravity law, we made the (implicitly) idealizing assumption that Earth was a large mass in a single point; that is, we idealized away the complications that arise from the fact that Earth is really an irregular ball with varying density. In the example of the spring-and-mass harmonic oscillator, we idealized away the fact that the surface on which the mass rests causes friction.

An idealized model may (but need not) approximate actual behavior in the world, but there will always be some error. We can reduce that error by releasing *seriatim* the idealized restrictions on the secondary factors: accounting for changes in g depending on where over Earth's surface

[8] Nowak (1980).

35

we drop our ball or for the damping effect of surface friction on the harmonic oscillator. Models with different combinations of secondary factors released form a family with natural hierarchies. To illustrate idealization in economic practice, Kees Cools et al. give a rather neat formal account of the well-known Modigliani-Miller theorem using Nowak's framework, showing the hierarchy of models that is generated as idealizing assumptions are relaxed.[9] The Modigliani-Miller theorem states that, in an idealized world, the ratio of debt to equity on a firm's balance sheet is irrelevant to the firm's value. Cools et al. list eleven idealizing assumptions, such as frictionless capital markets, no bankruptcy costs, and no taxes.[10]

The notion of idealization is, I think, an important one. It clarifies the power to make sense of the world that relatively simple models have, while at the same time respecting the idea that phenomena are complex. Cartwright's idea that controlled experiments produce robust phenomena through a process of shielding and particular interventions can be seen as the practical counterpart of isolating a theoretical relationship through idealizing assumptions. Yet Nowak's treatment of idealization seems incomplete to me. First, it is too formal in the sense that there is no functional distinction between primary and secondary factors. The interest in idealization is precisely that it isolates the essential, but whether something is essential is a question not of form, but of what reality is like. The danger is that without a notion of *essence*, idealization might be reduced either to a fancy name for an arbitrary selection of ceteris paribus conditions or to a formal

---

[9] Cools et al. (1994).   [10] Cools et al. (1994), pp. 211–12.

nesting relationship for theories. But I do not want to go further into this problem here.

There is a second difficulty in Nowak's account of idealization, which is also partly related to its formalism. The examples Nowak gives, and the example of the Modigliani-Miller theorem, presuppose a virtually complete account of a phenomenon in order to highlight the way in which idealizing assumptions isolate a particular aspect of it. If we had an exhaustively complete theory of the phenomenon, such that we could accurately specify each of the secondary factors that were set aside, then there would be no reason to draw the distinction between primary and secondary factors at all. Formally, we could always work out the implication of dropping any factor, so why would we regard some as more privileged than the others? And, what is more, why would we care? The practical reason for using idealized models is that we do not know all of the secondary factors that influence a phenomenon.

There is an analogue in experimental sciences. Often an experiment has to be shielded from outside influences: protected from radiation, light, magnetism, motion, and so forth. Yet, no matter how an experiment is shielded – that is, no matter how many secondary factors are set aside – there may always be another outside influence against which inadequate precaution was taken. Becquerel thought that he had shielded his photographic plate from outside influences but discovered radioactivity when he found out that his shielding was inadequate. Cartwright describes an experiment, the Stanford Gravity Probe, that attempts to shield against all outside influences.[11] The

---

[11] Cartwright (1989), pp. 66–71.

experimenters also adopt a strategy of constantly rotating the probe so that any unshielded influence will affect the apparatus symmetrically and cancel out. This is an implicit admission that they cannot guess what all the outside influences might be, much less shield the experiment completely. One point of randomized experiments is to induce this sort of cancellation of unshielded influences.

It is not too much of a stretch to regard Pissarides's model as an idealization. It does, however, present some formal problems. For example, the length of lives is set to two periods, which is not quite the same thing as eliminating the secondary factor by choosing an extreme value. It is not like, for example, idealizing our steel ball by assuming that it is colorless. It is like assuming that the ball is green, when it is really black. That probably does not signify for the question of the velocity of a falling object, but the length of a worker's life is a material variable in Pissarides's optimization problem.

Pissarides's does not use his model to draw sharp quantitative conclusions. A better example of an empirical idealized model is Finn Kydland and Edward Prescott's real-business-cycle model and its successors.[12] These are representative-agent models, usually with a single good and a single producer/consumer. The parameters are assigned values that are meant to be representative of facts about the economy. This is known as *calibration*. And then quantitative implications are drawn from the model. These are taken seriously enough by real-business-cycle modelers that they compare them, usually informally, to analogous variables in the world. It is as if Pissarides had

[12] Kydland and Prescott (1982); also see Hartley et al. (1997, 1998).

filled in the parameters of his model with numbers and generated numbers for J_t and q_t in equations (1.1) and (1.2), which he then compared to the actual values for u and v.

How do we know when our model has succeeded? We do not expect a perfect fit. Not on the dimensions of the secondary factors, because they were idealized away. And not on the dimensions of the primary factors, because the secondary factors must matter somehow if they are to be factors at all. What we hope is that the idealized model gets close enough to be useful. But how close is that? One answer is, closer than alternative models. That poses a number of nice questions about the standards on which we can assess *relative* success. This is a matter of great practical importance: if Keynesian, real-business-cycle, sunspot, and other idealized models describe the data somewhat similarly, how are we to choose among them? This is a question that cannot be answered at the level of methodology, but must in large part be addressed at the level of econometric and statistical technique. Methodology may, nevertheless, suggest general strategies and certainly can clarify the stakes. It is fair to say, as a practical matter, that there is a yawning gap between idealized business-cycle models and the empirical data that they are meant to explain.

ECONOMETRICS AND THE NOMOLOGICAL MACHINE

Let us return to the question, are macroeconomic models blueprints for nomological machines? I think that

Pissarides's model certainly is not. I could not build a real-world version of it. Is it a blueprint for an idealized nomological machine? On this, I am of two minds. Pissarides does not really present his model in that light. But among new classical business-cycle modelers, real-business-cycle modelers present models that are no less unrealistic as adequate explanations of macroeconomic fluctuations. Robert Lucas states the goal fairly clearly:

> One exhibits understanding of business cycles by constructing a *model* in the most literal sense: a fully articulated artificial economy which behaves through time so as to imitate closely the time series behavior of actual economics [*sic*].[13]

> Our task as I see it . . . somewhat more bluntly and operationally . . . is to write a FORTRAN program that will accept specific economic policy rules as "input" and will generate "output" statistics describing the operating characteristics of time series we care about.[14]

Kydland and Prescott and the other real-business-cycle modelers have taken Lucas's program to heart, but in full realization that their models are idealized, or in their more usual turn of phrase, *stylized*. So, we have to make a choice. We can reject the notion that macromodels are nomological machines at all, or follow Lucas and Kydland and Prescott and not only accept that the macromodels are idealized nomological machines but take their quantitative assessment seriously.

[13] Lucas (1977), p. 219.   [14] Lucas (1980).

It would be too facile to say: "Well, of course, a real-business-cycle model is not a nomological machine, because it is not an economy." No, it is not; yet, when cast as a simulation on a computer, it may be an *idealized* nomological machine in the sense that a toy locomotive is an idealization of a real locomotive. And a toy may stand in such a relationship to the real thing as to provide useful, even highly accurate information about its operation.

Cartwright's object in suggesting the notion of a nomological machine was to highlight the stringency and specificity of the requirements that are necessary to get robust, probabilistic empirical regularities to manifest themselves. She thinks that Pissarides's model illustrates her point because it makes so many highly particular assumptions to generate well-behaved probability distributions for q_t and J_t. I reject this view, because the chasm between Pissarides's model and the actual data is too wide. Cartwright, on the other hand, draws a quite different conclusion. She argues that typical econometric procedures, which do not impose controls as detailed or as stringent of those in Pissarides's models, are not candidates for nomological machines and cannot succeed in their objective of conveying information about the capacity of the model and its components.

Cartwright's specific example is a line of research described by Sudhir Anand and S. M. Ravi Kanbur using

the following model [in which] some measure of living standard, H_{it}, for country i and time t:

$$H_{it} = \alpha_t + \beta Y_{it} + \delta E_{it} + \lambda_i + u_{it}'',$$

where Y_{it} is per capita income; E_{it} is social welfare expenditure; α_t is a time-specific but country-invariant effect assumed to reflect technological advances (e.g. disease eradication techniques); λ_i is a country-specific and time-invariant "fixed effect"; δ is the marginal impact of social expenditure on living standards; and u_{it}'' is a random error term.[15]

The object of these studies is to measure δ or, at least, to better understand the relationship between E and H. Cartwright rejects such econometric research a priori on the grounds that one cannot imagine the different countries in this cross-section to be a nomological machine or the controls in the regression as providing an adequate enough shield to isolate the capacity supposedly measured by δ. This would be a devastating conclusion for econometrics; but, fortunately, Cartwright goes too far.

Recall that I said that the nomological machines raised two questions. The question to which Cartwright answered "yes" and I answer "no" is, are macroeconomic models blueprints for nomological machines? The other question, to which we would both answer "yes," is, are there nomological machines in macroeconomics? I believe that there are in economies real structures that generate robust, though highly special, empirical regularities. An important part of finding those regularities is in fact asking the question, do the data conform to what one would expect had they been generated by a nomological machine?

Let us illustrate this with a concrete example. Pissarides mentions that an implication of his analysis is that a plot of the unemployment and the vacancy rate should make

---

[15] Anand and Kanbur (1995), p. 321.

counterclockwise loops over the business cycle, the overall relationship (the Beveridge curve) between them being inverse.[16] Furthermore, he states that such loops are observed. Let us look at this question using some primitive econometrics.

Vacancy data is better for the United Kingdom than it is for the United States, but having easier access to U.S. data, I plotted a measure of help-wanted advertisements in newspapers against the unemployment rate for the United States, quarterly from 1951 (earliest available data) through 1986, retaining ten years of observations for checking stability. Figure 2.3 presents the scatterplot with a regression line. The data seem to indicate the relationship is not inverse as expected, but direct. These data certainly do not look like data from a well-defined chance set-up.

In Figure 2.4, I connect the data points in chronological sequence. They are not random. They show two patterns: loops, indicative of serial correlation, and a drift up and to the right, indicative of nonstationarity.

Figure 2.5 plots the two time series against the business cycle. Vacancies reach a high and unemployment a low near the peak of each business cycle. The extreme points drift higher with each cycle. Figure 2.6 plots data transformed by subtracting the value at the previous cyclical peak from each series eliminating the drift. Figure 2.7 is the scatterplot of this data with a fitted regression line, which is now clearly inverse. The data is still serially correlated, though the loops are now difficult to see since they are all centered on the regression line.

---

[16] Pissarides (1992), p. 1390.

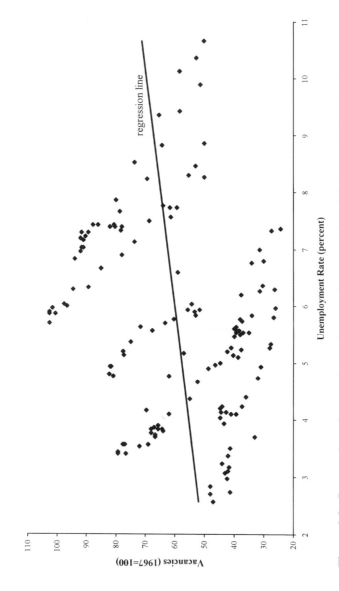

Figure 2.3. Scatterplot of vacancies and unemployment, 1951–86. *Source:* DRI Database Series: (LHEL) Index of help-wanted advertising in newspapers (1967 = 100; seasonally adjusted); (LHUR) Unemployment rate: all workers, 16 years and over (percent; seasonally adjusted).

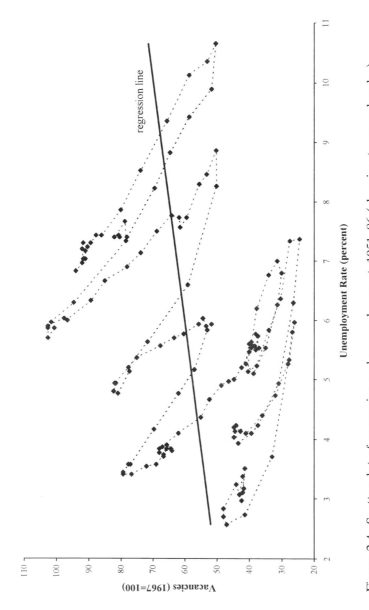

Figure 2.4. Scatterplot of vacancies and unemployment, 1951–86 (showing temporal order).
Source: see Figure 2.3.

45

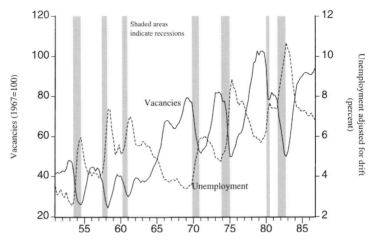

Figure 2.5. Vacancies, unemployment, and the business cycle, 1951–86. *Source*: see Figure 2.3.

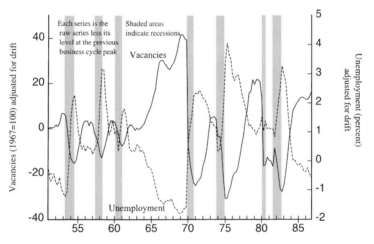

Figure 2.6. Cyclically adjusted vacancies, unemployment, and the business cycle, 1951–86. *Source*: see Figure 2.3.

46

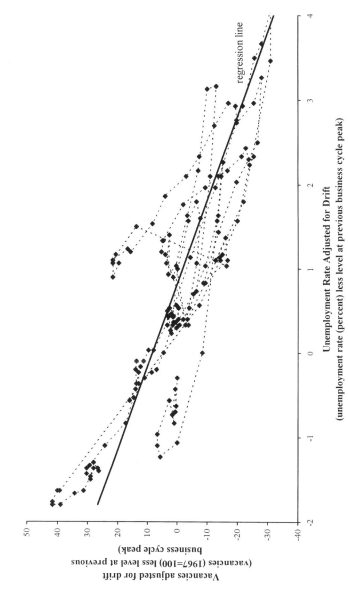

Figure 2.7. Cyclically adjusted vacancies and unemployment, 1951–86. *Source:* see Figure 2.3.

47

Is the relationship stable? Figure 2.8 plots the data from 1951 to 1996. A formal test of stability rejects the constancy of the regression coefficients. Nevertheless, comparison of Figures 2.7 and 2.8 suggest that, as a coarse, economic regularity, the relationship is robust. The regression slopes are not very different, and there is no dramatic change in the scatter of the points. Elimination of the trends from the two series and their positive long-run associations clearly reveals an inverse relationship, but it does not eliminate the serial correlation – the loops remain. Figure 2.9 plots a representative loop, from the 1981 to 1990 business cycle (peak to peak) in which the counterclockwise pattern is evident. The relationship appears to be stable.

This exercise is econometrics of a very primitive sort. It exemplifies pretty well the kind of econometrics that was done in the period before electronic computers.[17] It differs in detail, not in spirit, from the econometrics discussed in Pissarides's article and from much of the econometrics currently practiced.

We have uncovered three robust facts about unemployment and vacancies:

1. they trend together in the long run;
2. they are inversely related for any business cycle;
3. their relationship is nonlinear (the loops).

These facts are robust, but they are imprecise. From comparing Figure 2.3 and Figure 2.8 we see that Cartwright is perfectly right: what we observe are complex products of

---

[17] See Hendry and Morgan (1995), Morgan (1990), Klein (1996).

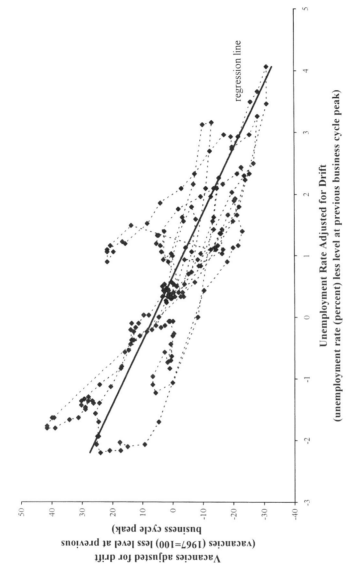

Figure 2.8. Cyclically adjusted vacancies and unemployment, 1951–96. *Source:* see Figure 2.3.

49

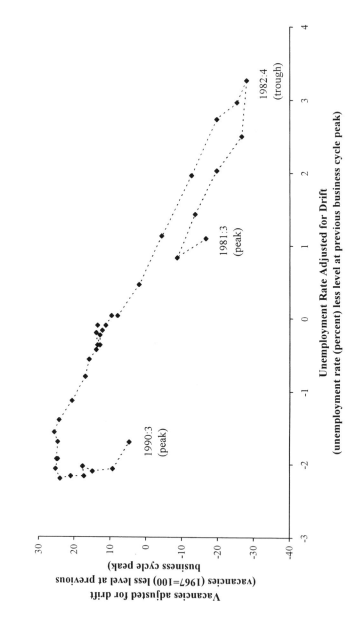

Figure 2.9. Cyclically adjusted vacancies and unemployment over the business cycle, 1981:3 (peak) to 1990:3 (peak). *Source*: see Figure 2.3.

deeper interactions. The superficial conjunctions of data, if they show any pattern at all, may be profoundly misleading. To discover what the enduring relationships are requires interventions or, at least, accounting for conflating factors, as we did in controlling for the trend in going from Figure 2.4 to Figure 2.7. The control here was of a rather unspecific kind, unlike the hyperfine assumptions of the nomological machine. We set aside the trend movements without shedding any light on what factors govern the trend. We were guided by an economic intuition that some economic relations are more likely to be stable within a business cycle than from one cycle to another. There were no guarantees. It worked; but it might not have.

We have not found a covering law or directly exhibited the capacity of a nomological machine. On general economic grounds, it is more likely that the relationship between unemployment and vacancies results from a common cause rather than from one causing the other directly.[18] Yet, it may nevertheless be useful to know this noncausal correlation. It is probably not a bad guide to newspaper managers of the demand for

---

[18] Unlike the equations that usually represent them, regressions are directed. In a causal context, one would treat the independent variables as causes of the dependent variable. If I am right – that unemployment and vacancies are correlated because of a common causes – then there is no reason to prefer the regression of vacancies on unemployment, which is the regression line in the diagrams, to one of unemployment on vacancies. The former minimizes the variance of the error measured as deviations between the regression line and observed vacancies, the latter as deviations between the regression line and observed unemployment. The fitted curves have different slopes, although they are qualitatively similar.

advertisements conditional on forecasts of the unemployment rate.

Despite the ambitions and rhetoric of the Cowles Commission, econometrics is rarely about the measurement of completely articulated causal systems – that is, about quantifying the parameters of a nomological machine.[19] It is about observation.[20] Observations invite explanation. Even if a fact, such as the relationship of unemployment to vacancies, were to vanish, its having been so now stands in need of explanation.

The robustness of econometric facts is an argument for the existence of nomological machines, but the tools for discovering those facts do not presuppose (fully articulated) knowledge of the construction of those machines. The existence of robust facts is always contingent. Consider the attempts, described by Anand and Kanbur, to determine the effect of social expenditure on economic welfare in Sri Lanka.[21] There may be good economic reasons to doubt that this can be measured accurately by situating Sri Lanka in a cross-country study that presupposes that each country in the study is the outcome of a common process. Anand and Kanbur implicitly reason that, if there is enough commonality of structure among the countries in the study (if the data are examples of the successful operation of a nomological machine), then the data will have certain econometrically observable features. When that proves not to be the case, they conclude that the cross-sectional investigation is fruitless and move on to a time-series study of Sri Lanka alone. Realistic meta-

---

[19] Morgan (1990), pp. 251–58.   [20] Cf. Hoover (1994).
[21] Anand and Kanbur (1995).

physics could not have told us a priori that they were right to do so.

Nor can I agree with the message implicit in Cartwright's work that the conditions under which econometrics could succeed are too demanding to be met. The goal of econometrics is not to serve as a nomological machine nor as its blueprint, but to discover facts that are generated by unobservable nomological machines, facts that theoretical models explain by providing rough drawings, if not blueprints. The situation is like that encountered by British code breakers during World War II. There were intercepted messages (data); patterns were discovered in the messages (econometrics); a design emerged for a machine that could generate such patterns, starting with a general conceptualization (an idealized theoretical model) and ending with a working model (a goal that for many practical, and perhaps metaphysical, reasons may be beyond economics).

ONCE AGAIN: ARE THERE LAWS IN ECONOMICS?

When one thinks about it, the idea of scientific laws employs an odd metaphor. Laws in civil society are norms to which we may or may not conform. And we have erected the vast apparatus of police, lawyers, courts, and prisons to deal with the consequences of some of us failing to conform. But scientific laws are thought to be unbreakable. While we condemn (or, on rare occasions, praise) those who violate civil laws, we usually regard as absurd those who propose to do something that we believe violates a law of nature. Cartwright and others have done us a great service by knocking the idea of the universal scope of natural laws down a peg. Yet, for the most part, they continue to engage in talk of scientific laws. I think, however, that they have made a strong case that "law talk" is dispensable in physics. And even if not dispensable in physics, it seems to do nothing in economics. In economics we would do much better to concentrate on models and their relationships to the world. It is, in practice, what we do; and it is an enterprise that should be granted both greater respect and greater critical attention.

SUGGESTED READINGS

A good introduction to the covering-law model is found in Carl Hempel's "Laws and Their Role in Scientific Explanation" (reprinted in Richard Boyd, Philip Gaspar, and J. D. Trout, eds., *The Philosophy of Science*. Cambridge, MA: MIT Press, 1991).

Nancy Cartwright's views on the limitations of econometrics can be found in various articles and, particularly, in her book *The Dappled World* (Cambridge: Cambridge University Press, 1999). Although I criticize her account of econometrics, most of her splendid book is highly sympathetic to the views I express in this volume.

A good introduction to Leszek Nowak's account of idealization is found in his and Izabella Nowakowa's "On Correspondence between Economic Theories," pp. 135–46 (in Bert Hamminga and Neil B. De Marchi, eds., *Idealiza-*

tion VI: Idealization in Economics, Poznan Studies in the Philosophy of Science, no. 38, 1994). The same volume contains a particularly lucid example of how the idealization strategy can be applied to economics – in this case, to the well-known Modigliani-Miller theorem; this is the article by Kees Cools, Bert Hamminga, and Theo A. F. Kuipers, "Truth Approximation by Concretization in Capital Structure Theory," pp. 205–28.

While innocent of philosophical intentions, Finn Kydland and Edward Prescott's seminal real-business-cycle model, found in their article "Time to Build and Aggregate Fluctuations," *Econometrica* 50(6) (1982), 1345–69, is a clear example of a quantified, though nonetheless idealized, model in macroeconomics.

3

Does Macroeconomics Need Microfoundations?

Does Macroeconomics Need Microfoundations?

As I observed in the first lecture, I chose Pissarides's model as a paradigm of the modern macroeconomic model for a variety of reasons: the clarity of its goals and exposition; the manner in which it attempted to relate its theoretical construction to empirical facts (at least in principle); and, by no means the least important reason, because it was the model that Nancy Cartwright held up as an example of a nomological machine in economics. A number of fellow economists, however, question whether Pissarides's model really is a *macroeconomic* model. Because it appears to model the decision problem of the individual worker and the individual firm, some economists regard it as a microeconomic model. But this is all the better for my purposes because there is a persistent refrain in recent macroeconomics that the only acceptable macroeconomic models are those that have adequate *microfoundations*.

The idea of microfoundations did not originate with the new classical macroeconomics, but the manner in which the new classical macroeconomics has dominated the agenda of macroeconomics over the past quarter century has firmly cemented it in the minds of virtually all economists. Lucas puts it clearly when he longs for an economics that does not need the prefixes "micro" or "macro" – sound economics is held to be microeconomics, and any macroeconomics that is not just a shorthand for the manner in which microeconomics is applied to certain problems is held to be bad economics.[1]

Lucas advocates the euthanasia of macroeconomics and has spent most of his career supplying pills to hasten the demise of the once proud models of the macroeconomic

[1] Lucas (1987), pp. 107–108.

era. It has taken time, but we have reached the point at which there are graduate students for whom John Hicks's IS/LM model is just a dim memory from an undergraduate textbook and whose first lecture in their graduate macroeconomics courses began with a Hamiltonian describing the dynamic optimization problem of what appears to be an individual agent. Gradually, undergraduate textbooks are following suit, and even the econometric forecasting models of the United States Federal Reserve System have undergone surgery to remove the IS/LM model that once was the beating heart of their more than two hundred equation system. That the profession has sworn allegiance to the ideal of microfoundations is beyond doubt. The question before us is whether they are right to do so.

SOME HISTORY

The earliest empirical economics is macroeconomics. The word "economics" derives from a Greek word meaning the management of the household. The earliest name for our subject, "political economy," consciously drew the analogy between the management of the household and the management of the state. But the politics of the seventeenth and eighteenth centuries was somewhat different from the politics of the nineteenth, twentieth, and twenty-first centuries. The transition to individualism was incomplete, and it was not uncommon for the political theorists of the day to think more of the social hierarchy as king, aristocracy, merchants, farmers, peasants, and so forth with little regard to the role of the individual. The early statistical researches of William Petty, Gregory King, and Charles Davenant were aimed not at understanding the economic behavior of particular people but at determining the capacities of England and Ireland to support the military ambitions of the English king. The models of François Quesnay and the Physiocrats, which bear many structural and methodological resemblances to modern macroeconomic models, went a step further. Again, appealing to the division of French society into broad classes (nobility, farmers, artisans), they gave normative advice to the French king on how to direct the economy in a manner that would enlarge his military capabilities.

The macroeconomic models of the seventeenth and eighteenth centuries were not supplanted all at once in a wave of individualism. The seeds had to be planted. The beginning of wisdom was the notion promoted by Adam Smith and the great Scottish political economists that the source of social welfare was the individual welfare of the ordinary man. We are so used to the idea that economics is about harnessing individual self-interest for social harmony and to attributing this idea to Smith, that we forget how limited were his claims for individualism. We remember the "Invisible Hand," but this image appears only once in the *Wealth of Nations*, in the context of foreign trade (and in two other instances in Smith's noneconomic works). Bernard Mandeville, early in the eighteenth century, in *The Fable of the Bees*, put the point that private vice (greed) could promote public virtue far more clearly than did Smith. But Smith took a dim view of Mandeville. Smith, David Ricardo, and the other classical economists were mainly concerned with market phenomena, and the individual played a relatively weak analytical and empirical role in their arguments.

With marginalism in the middle of the nineteenth century, the analytical ground shifts more clearly to the individual, but market phenomena remain the focus of William Stanley Jevons and the English political economists. It is in the work of the French economists Augustin Cournot and Leon Walras that the individual is truly made the analytical center of economics and the problem of how individuals coordinate socially, usually ascribed to Smith, takes center stage.

The political philosophy of the late nineteenth century is marked by debates over the relative explanatory role of individualism versus superindividual categories. Marxists led the way. For them, classes determine men, rather than men determining classes. (Yet, one should note that Karl Marx's economics owed its analytical framework to Smith and Ricardo and so was tainted, at least as far as they went with it, by individualism.) Austrian economics presented a clear contrast in which Carl Menger and, in the twentieth century, Ludwig von Mises, Friedrich von Hayek, and others espoused *methodological individualism*: the doctrine that the only well-grounded explanations of social phenomena were ones that appealed to the actions and behaviors of individuals.

English and American economics maintained an incomplete individualism. Although Alfred Marshall managed to kill the "political" that had long modified "economy" in the name of our discipline, his object was more to refocus attention on the analytics of the subject rather than on the applications. (The term "political economy" has been reborn in the past twenty years, though it conveys a very different sense now than it did in Smith's time.) Marshall discussed the particular firm and the particular worker or consumer. But, like his English and Scottish forefathers, he did so mainly to illuminate markets. The analyzed individual is meant to typify individuals in general. It is to Marshall, with his discussion of the "representative firm," that we owe the idea of the *representative agent*.[2] Still, Marshall's markets are not economy-wide, but are focused on particular products. Economics by 1930 appears mainly to be microeconomics. Yet, the proto-macroeconomics of the earlier time did not completely vanish. It is clearly evident in theoretical discussions of money, especially of the quantity theory, which never succeeded in finding adequate grounding in individual analysis. And it is evident in empirical discussions of business cycles, which were regarded as economy-wide phenomena.

So things stood in the mid-1930s, when John Maynard Keynes was writing the *General Theory*. Keynes did not invent macroeconomics, nor did he use the term. (As far as I can discover, Ragnar Frisch was the first to use the term, in 1931, though it became current only after the Second World War.)[3] Keynes, nevertheless, clarified the distinction between what we now call macroeconomics and microeconomics and made it possible for us to ask the question, how are the two related? As is evident in his discussion of the consumption function (the marginal propensity to consume follows from a "fundamental

[2] Marshall's notion is, as we will see, substantially different from that common in modern macroeconomics; see Hartley (1996, 1997).

[3] Frisch used the term in his lectures; Erik Lindahl may have been the first to use it in print in 1939; see Fitoussi and Velupillai (1993).

psychological law"), investment (entrepreneurs optimize with respect to opportunity costs), and the demand for money (speculators anticipate capital gains or losses), Keynes follows Marshall in looking to the individual decision problem for illumination. These appeals to individual behavior remain in the service of aggregate explanations. Despite the fact – largely ignored in potted histories – that he stresses the heterogeneity of individual responses as a central feature of aggregate behavior, Keynes never explores the relationship between the individual and the aggregate in any really systematic way.

Microeconomics so dominated economic thinking in 1936 that the cry for microfoundations for the newly resurgent macroeconomics was almost immediate. Jacob Viner and Wassily Leontief wrote microeconomic criticisms of the *General Theory*.[4] Lawrence Klein, in his *Keynesian Revolution*, thought it necessary to discuss the microeconomic underpinnings of the principal Keynesian aggregate functions.[5] The history of the first twenty-five years of postwar macroeconomics is largely the hanging of microeconomic flesh on the skeleton of interpretation of Keynes's *General Theory* formalized in Hicks's aggregate general-equilibrium, IS/LM model. James Dusenberry, Milton Friedman, and Franco Modigliani tried to explain the microeconomics of consumption; William Baumol and James Tobin, the demand for money; Dale Jorgenson, investment; Don Patinkin, labor; and so forth.[6]

---

[4] Viner (1936) and Leontief (1936).   [5] Klein (1947).
[6] Dusenberry (1949), Friedman (1957), Modigliani and Brumberg (1954), Baumol (1952), Tobin (1956, 1958), Jorgenson (1963), and Patinkin (1965).

Does Macroeconomics Need Microfoundations?

Beginning with Robert Clower's dual-decision hypothesis and Robert Barro and Herschel Grossman's fixed-price models, the urge for microfoundations began to infect the general-equilibrium framework.[7] It is no longer enough that each function have an individualistic foundation; since individuals are assumed to be making choices to generate each function separately, those choices really ought to be coordinated and consistent. This is a hard problem with heterogeneous agents. The modern representative agent, which is essentially a homogeneity assumption, made his appearance first in these models. At more or less the same time, Lucas and Leonard Rapping began to model unemployment as an optimization problem. Lucas made consistent optimization in general equilibrium the centerpiece of his monetary model published in the *Journal of Economic Theory* in 1972.[8] Strictly speaking, this model is not a representative-agent model. Yet, it is highly idealized and assumes that all individuals are fundamentally identical. From there, it is only a short step to the representative-agent models that have dominated new classical macroeconomics since the early 1970s.

REDUCTIONISM

So much for a brief history of the movement for microfoundations in economics. What are the intellectual roots of this urge to ground macroeconomics in the individual? It has analogies in other sciences. The nature of scientific

---

[7] Clower (1965) and Barro and Grossman (1971).   [8] Lucas (1972).

explanation is a hotly debated subject among philosophers and scientists. One plausible view is that a theory is explanatory when it achieves parsimony: if a complex phenomenon can be reduced to some smaller number of governing principles, then we regard the complex phenomenon as having been explained.

In the eighteenth century the ideal gas laws were formulated. The Boyle-Charles law states that

$$pV = nRT,$$

where p is pressure, V is volume, n is the number of moles of the gas, R is the universal gas constant, and T is temperature. As the name suggests this law is an idealization of the results of empirical observations and holds with a high degree of accuracy at moderate temperatures and low pressures.

The gas law appears to be an approximate truth about physical reality, but nevertheless physicists were not happy with its sui generis quality. The solution is found in the kinetic theory of gases, which provides an account of the gas laws as a deduction from Newtonian mechanics. The kinetic theory is also based on an idealization: the gas is assumed to be composed of molecules regarded as perfectly elastic point masses. With the added assumption that the velocities of the molecules are distributed according to a particular random distribution – that they are equally likely to move in every direction – it is possible to derive the gas laws. Temperature corresponds to the mean energy of the molecules and pressure to the mean momentum transferred by contact with the walls of the containing vessel. The kinetic theory of gases thus constitutes a *reduction* of the macrophysical gas laws to the microphysical Newtonian mechanics.

Notice two features of this reduction. The first is that it is not micro all the way down. In addition to Newton's laws, the kinetic theory relies on a statistical assumption – that is, an implicitly macro assumption. Also, notice that the categories that apply to Newton's laws and to the gas laws are very different. A single molecule has momentum and energy, but it does not have pressure or temperature. To make the derivation work, it is necessary to identify aggregate properties of the collection of molecules (their *average* energy and momentum) as corresponding to the macro properties (temperature and pressure) that have quite different sensible characteristics. The phenomena of temperature and pressure can be thought of as *emergent properties* of the aggregation of molecules.

Reductionist strategies are pursued throughout science. Recently, in biology, a lot of effort has been directed to reducing macrobiological phenomena to the micro principles of genetics and organic chemistry. But even here, the effort is controversial, with one wag saying: "the only way to reduce biology to chemistry is through death."[9] The philosophical mind/body problem has, in the age of neuroscience, also generated a debate over reductionism. The issue is whether mental states can be completely explained by knowledge of brain states. Even if they could, the issue of the phenomenological difference

---

[9] Vercelli (1991), p. 243.

between the two levels is larger here than it is with respect to the gas laws. Seeing a beautiful woman does not seem to be the same kind of thing as any pattern of neuron firings. Vision and, to a greater degree, aesthetic appreciation appear to be emergent properties, even if there is a reduction.

The situation is even more complex than that. You and I can see the same thing even though our brain states are not the same. Similarly, you can see the same thing at different times even though your brain state is different at each time. There is no one-to-one mapping between the macro phenomena of mind and the micro phenomena of brain states. This observation has led to the notion of *supervenience*. Mental states are said to supervene on brain states in the sense that any time one could exactly reproduce a certain brain state and collateral conditions, the same mental state would occur, even though that mental state may occur for other configurations of brain states as well, and even though the appropriate phenomenological descriptions of the mental state are completely different from those of the brain states. Supervenience guarantees the autonomy of the macro level in the sense that it ensures that one can rationally use an independent language and categories to describe the macro level and that one should not expect to find unique deductions from the micro to the macro. Yet, it also underscores the connection between the micro and the macro: no macro state exists unless an appropriate micro state exists. Supervenience has been offered both as a way of eliminating the need for reduction and as a justification for a weaker form of reduction. Which way one looks at it partly depends on what one views as threatened.

ECONOMICS AND METHODOLOGICAL INDIVIDUALISM

So what about reductionism in economics? Whether economic explanations must be reductive depends in part on how one defines economics. An older tradition defines it with respect to certain areas of human life. The classic definitions can be summarized in a word: *plutology*, the science of wealth. John Stuart Mill writes:

> Writers on Political Economy profess to teach, or to investigate, the nature of Wealth, and the laws of its production and distribution: including, directly or remotely, the operation of all the causes which the condition of mankind, or of any society of human beings, in respect to this universal object of human desire, is made prosperous or the reverse.[10]

Similarly, Alfred Marshall writes:

> Political Economy or Economics is a study of mankind in the ordinary business of life; it examines that part of individual and social action which is most closely connected with the attainment and with the use of the material requisites of wellbeing.
>
> Thus it is on the one side a study of wealth; and on the other, and more important side, a part of the study of man.[11]

[10] Mill (1848/1911), p. 1. [11] Marshall (1920), p. 1.

Modern economists almost all follow the much different definition of Lionel Robbins:

> Economics is the science which studies human behaviour as a relationship between ends and scarce means which have alternative uses.[12]

Economics is, in Robbins's view, the science of choice. Economics is, in modern terminology, microeconomics.

Once microeconomics is seen as defining the very nature of economics, any macroeconomic phenomenon will be seen to need a reductive explanation. Of course, it is one thing to want such an explanation and quite another to have it. It is obviously impractical to dispense with measurements of temperature and pressure and to keep track of the velocities of each and every molecule even in a relatively small volume of gas. Similarly, it is absurd to think that practical economics can trace the decisions and constraints facing each individual agent in the economy. I call this the *Cournot problem*, because the first clear statement of it is found in Cournot's *Researches into the Mathematical Principles of the Theory of Wealth* (1838). No one really denies the Cournot problem; the only question is what to do about it.

Notice that the motivations for seeking a reduction are different in economics than they are in biological sciences. Biologists are suspicious, for instance, of mental explanations because they involve *intentional* states: beliefs, purposes, desires, will, goals, and so forth. Human mental life

---

[12] Robbins (1935), p. 16.

is *teleological*; that is, it is directed to ends. The reduction of the mental to the neurological is appealing to scientists precisely because neurons, chemicals, molecules, genes, and such do not have ends or intentional states. Reduction banishes teleology. In economics, it is just the reverse. Macroeconomic relations, say as represented in Okun's law, which relates changes in the unemployment rate to the growth rate of gross domestic product (GDP), are not obviously intentional anymore than the gas laws are. But if macroeconomic relations are regarded as the products of human action, this could be seen as a defect. The goal of reducing macroeconomics to microeconomics is to recapture human intentions. Reduction reclaims teleology.

The difference is clear in what is probably the most influential paper in macroeconomics in the postwar period: Lucas's "Econometric Policy Evaluation: A Critique."[13] Lucas criticized the empirical macroeconomics of the day – especially the large-scale macroeconometric forecasting models – on the basis that their equations captured transitory correlations in the data that would not remain stable in the face of changes in policy regimes. His idea is that people make choices subject to constraints that include their best expectations of government policy. If the government uses the macroeconomic models to guide its policy choices, it will surely find that the models fail as soon as it changes its policy, because agents will adapt to the constraints of the new policy. Projecting macroeconomic relationships estimated in the past into the future implicitly assumes that the policy of the past continues. But

[13] Lucas (1976).

if the government uses those projections to guide changes in its policy, then it assumes that people expect the old policy, even while a new policy is in place. People are not stupid, so the past projections are bound to fail. The most common response to the Lucas critique (for example, in the program of Lars Peter Hansen and Thomas Sargent and, more recently, in real-business-cycle models) was to argue that economic projections would be secure only if they were grounded in a deep analysis of the decision problems faced by individuals, including their detailed understanding of the structure of policy.[14] A model was said to be secure from the Lucas critique only if it was grounded in relationships built up from the "deep parameters" corresponding to tastes and technology. Only well-specified optimization problems were supposed to provide a secure basis for economic prediction. In other words, macroeconomics must be reduced to microeconomics. The conviction that macroeconomics must possess microfoundations has changed the face of the discipline in the last quarter century.

That the argument for microfoundations should have been so successful rhetorically is, I think, puzzling. For it ignores the obvious difficulties in empirical implementation posed by the Cournot problem. As I said before, no one believes that economists can practically trace the decision problems of millions of individuals and aggregate them to discover macroeconomic behavior. The intellectual triumph of microfoundations is grounded not in methodological individualism (that is, in a strategy of basing all empirical explanations on the behavior of indi-

---

[14] Hansen and Sargent (1980).

viduals) but in *ontological individualism* (the conviction that the only real entities in the economy are individuals). Who could disagree with that?

Well, I would. Unfortunately, the full argument for this position would take us further down a metaphysical byway than any group of economists is likely to want to go. Still, I would at least like to poke a few holes in the presumption that ontological individualism is necessarily correct. The fear of the ontological individualist is that if he says that macroeconomic entities like GDP or the general price level are real, he must also say that they are independent of the individual people who constitute the economy. The second claim is, of course, obviously wrong, but ontological individualism does not follow from denying it.

The relationship between microeconomics and macroeconomics could be one of supervenience. Any identical reconfiguration of the agents in the economy and their situations results in the same configuration of the macroeconomic entities in the economy, but the mapping is not one to one. What is more, the supervenience of the macroeconomy on the microeconomy is not just a weak form of reductionism. This is because of intentionality at the microlevel. Individuals have to make plans and decisions on the basis of expectations about the future. In so doing, they face precisely the same problem that is faced by the economist from his detached perspective: the economy is too complex for a detailed microeconomic account to inform the construction of expectations. Individuals, just like economists, face the Cournot problem. When I try to figure out how much money to put aside to pay for my daughters' college education, I must make guesses about future inflation and interest rates, as well as about my own income. I cannot do that by constructing a realistic computable-general-equilibrium model of the economy. Instead, I use simple macroeconomic models (indeed, crude time-series models, such as one that says that future interest rates will be the average of past interest rates). But this means that I cannot completely reduce macro-economics to microeconomics. Microeconomics of the real world necessarily uses macroeconomic models and concepts as an input. The macroeconomy supervenes on the microeconomy but is not reducible to it.

AGGREGATION AND THE ILLUSION OF
A MICROECONOMIC ONTOLOGY

While I am convinced that the impulse that made the microfoundational argument succeed is ontological and not methodological, it would be absurd not to acknowledge the methodological sea change in macroeconomics after the Lucas critique. Macroeconomic models look like microeconomic models (hence the reaction that my use of Pissarides's model provoked among my colleagues). The same techniques, the same mathematics, the same language is used. But this is truly puzzling. The physicist who has successfully reduced the ideal gas laws to the kinetic theory of gases does not then abandon the language of pressure, temperature, and volume when working with gases or try to use momentum, mass, and velocity as the principal phenomenological categories for discussing the macroscopic behavior of gases.

74

But economists have taken a different tack. They have typically started with the microeconomics of the individual and then asked to what degree the lessons learned at that level can still apply to aggregates of individuals. There is, in consequence, a vast literature on the theory of aggregation. The general conclusion of this literature is that aggregation in which the macro looks like the micro can occur only under circumstances so stringent that they could never be fulfilled in the real world except by the merest chance. I want to argue something even stronger than that; namely, that even what appears to be perfect aggregation under ideal circumstances fails. But, first, let us consider the lessons of aggregation theory as they stand.

Economics is about heterogeneous things. In microeconomics we choose how to allocate our consumption among different goods or how to allocate factors of production used to make those goods. In both cases, we consider physical things of disparate natures and somehow have to make them equivalent. The role of utility functions or profit functions is to give us a common denominator, a basis for choosing among goods that otherwise are little alike. Similarly, when we calculate nominal GDP, we cannot add up the disparate goods until we have given them a common denominator – typically, money. Real GDP is even one step further removed, as we correct the monetary unit of measurement for changes in its own value by constructing a notion of a *general* price level.

Now, the first question asked in aggregation theory is, when is aggregation perfect? – that is, when can two disparate goods be added together and treated analytically as if they were but one good? The criteria are typically economic, not physical, though the first example may seem physical. Suppose that we have a certain quantity of coal and a certain quantity of oil. Coal and oil differ on many dimensions; but, if the only difference of material importance to us is the amount of heat they produce (which dimensions matter is the economic criterion), then we can measure each in British Thermal Units (BTUs), rather than in tons or barrels, and add them up in those units. This is the case in which, up to a factor of proportionality, the goods are perfect substitutes. Similarly, in any case in which goods are perfect substitutes on the relevant dimensions, we can aggregate them.

Oddly, the polar opposite case works as well. Consider the manufacture of water through burning hydrogen and oxygen. It takes exactly two moles of hydrogen and one mole of oxygen to make one mole of water. We cannot vary the formula. Hydrogen and oxygen are not substitutable; they are perfect complements. But we can aggregate perfectly by counting bundles of hydrogen and oxygen into bundles: $2H + 1O = 1$ water bundle.

Generally, however, except in these extreme cases, perfect aggregation is not possible. The reason is economic. If goods are neither perfect complements (in which case no change in the mix of the goods is possible) nor perfect substitutes (in which case no change in the mix of goods matters), then the mix of goods can be changed and still yield the same output or utility. How that mix changes depends on relative prices. As the price of a good rises, we purchase less of that good and more of its substitute. This is the basis for the common claim, going back to Hicks, that we can treat bundles of goods as composite commodities, so long as their relative prices do not change: the so-called *composite commodity theorem*.[15]

The composite commodity theorem is true as far as it goes, but notice how special are the assumptions on which it is based. We generally regard prices not as exogenous variables given outside the economic system, but as one of the important products of economic coordination. The proofs of the existence of a general equilibrium, going back to Kenneth Arrow and Gerard Debreu, demonstrate that there is a set of prices that coordinates economic activity. The prices are not themselves parameters, but change as the true parameters (tastes and technology, if we go back to Lucas's formulation) change. The composite commodity theorem, therefore, holds only when the relevant underlying parameters do not change. How relevant can that be for interesting economic analysis?

Let us illustrate the problem with an extremely simple example. Consider an economy with two consumers and two goods. These goods can be either two goods in a single period or one physical good that can be consumed in two different periods. It does not matter which interpretation we take for the example to work, although the second one is directly relevant to a number of intertemporal macroeconomic models. Let each individual (i) choose the goods (c_1 and c_2) by maximizing a Cobb-Douglas utility function:

$$u^i = \log c_1^i + \alpha^i \log c_2^i \tag{3.1}$$

subject to a budget constraint

[15] Hicks (1946), p. 46.

$$y^i - c_1^i - pc_2^i = 0, \qquad (3.2)$$

where y is exogenously given income, and p is the price of good 2 in terms of the numeraire, good 1. The demand for good 1 is

$$c_1^i = \frac{y^i}{1+\alpha^i}. \qquad (3.3)$$

Letting the superscripted, lower-case letters designate variables that apply to individual agents and upper-case or unsuperscripted letters, variables that apply to aggregates, the idea of the representative-agent model is simple. If equation (3.3) gives the demand for the individual for good 1, then the aggregate demand for good 1 is

$$C_1 = \frac{Y}{1+\alpha}. \qquad (3.4)$$

But, in our simple economy of only two agents, it is easy to check exactly what the aggregate form of the demand for good 1 should be. It is merely the sum of the two individual demands, so that

$$C_1 = c_1^1 + c_2^1 = \frac{y^1}{1+\alpha^1} + \frac{y^2}{1+\alpha^2} = \frac{(1+\alpha^1)y^1 + (1+\alpha^2)y^2}{(1+\alpha^1)(1+\alpha^2)}$$

$$= \frac{Y + \alpha^1 y^1 + \alpha^2 y^2}{(1+\alpha^1)(1+\alpha^2)}, \qquad (3.5)$$

since $Y = y^1 + y^2$. In general, equation (3.5) does not have the same form as equation (3.4). In fact, the only circumstances in which (3.4) and (3.5) are identical in form is when $\alpha^1 = \alpha^2 = \alpha$ – that is, when all agents have identical tastes.

As a rule, the conditions are even more stringent than that. I purposely chose a very tractable utility function. The Cobb-Douglas utility function is homothetic; that is, its indifference curves are each parallel blowups of the indifference curves closer to the origin. Equivalently, the income-expansion paths (that is, the locus of tangencies between indifference curves and budget constraints as the budget constraint is moved outward to reflect increasing income and constant relative prices) are all straight lines through the origin. And this is what the theorists tells us: some technical details and caveats to one side, perfect aggregation from individual agents to a representative agent requires that all agents have identical utility functions and that these be homothetic. Why? Because in these cases, income distribution is not relevant. Because of homotheticity, the ratios of goods consumed by any one individual remain the same whether that individual is rich or poor. And because utility functions are identical, the ratios of goods consumed are the same for any individual. In such circumstances, for a fixed aggregate income, redistributing that income among the individual consumers will not affect demands for individual goods and, therefore, will not affect relative prices. In that case, the conditions of Hicks's composite commodity theorem apply, and we can add up individual quantities to form economy-wide aggregates without loss of information.

Although the example that we have looked at is extremely simple, it carries a very general message. The conditions of exact aggregation are strong and almost certainly never fulfilled in any practical instance. Why should one accept the representative-agent model and the facile analogy from the micro to the macro? Indeed, recently, a number of economists – Rolf Mantel, Hugo Sonnenschein, and Debreu – have shown that theoretically there is no such analogy.[16] No matter how well behaved the microeconomic functions may be, the aggregate functions, given distributional variations, are essentially unrestricted and need not take a form that is derivable in any simple way from the form of the underlying micro functions. This means, for example, that if every underlying production function is Cobb-Douglas, there is no theoretical reason to conclude that the aggregate production will also be Cobb-Douglas. Conversely, if the aggregate production function for an economy is Cobb-Douglas (which to a first approximation it appears to be for the U.S. economy), there is no reason to believe that this tells us anything at all about the shape of the underlying production functions.

There is a strong belief, expressed not only in the ordinary practice of macroeconomics but in the methodological writings of philosophers of economics, that aggregation does not alter the fundamental categories of economics. Whereas in physics molecules have one sort of description and gases, even though they are aggregations of molecules, quite another, in economics real GDP is much like any other real good. Uskali Mäki makes the point I wish to oppose by saying that economics does not add to the "ontic furniture" of the world given to common sense.[17] This is, I think, an illusion that arises because of the view that perfect aggregation represents a possible limiting case of actual aggregation. The possibility of perfect aggrega-

---

[16] Kirman (1992) and Hartley(1997).   [17] Mäki (1996).

tion suggests the analogy of real GDP to an individual good. If, for example, relative prices are constant (that is, P_j/P_k is constant for all j and k), then $\sum_{j=1}^{n} P_{j,t}Q_{j,t}$ (where the t in the subscript indicates the base time, period t) can be normalized by choosing the units for the $Q_{j,t}$ so that each $P_{j,t} = 1$. Then, nominal GDP at time n can be written

$$\sum_{j=1}^{n} P_{j,t+n}Q_{j,t+n} = P_{t+n}\sum_{j=1}^{n} Q_{j,t+n}. \tag{3.6}$$

Under the assumed conditions P is unique. Some conclude, therefore, that in this limited case, one can treat the summation on the right-hand side of equation (3.6) as a natural aggregate quantity analogous to an individual quantity. The conditions for constant relative prices are almost certainly never fulfilled; but, even if they were, the summation is not analogous to an individual quantity. The general price level P in (3.6) still has the dimension period-n dollars/period-t (i.e., base period) dollars. To sum heterogeneous goods, they must still be converted to a common denominator, and in this case, the summation still has the dimensions of period-t dollars. This would be more perspicuous if (3.6) were written as

$$\sum_{j=1}^{n} P_{j,t+n}Q_{j,t+n} = P_{t+n}\sum_{j=1}^{n} 1_{j,t+n}Q_{j,t+n}, \tag{3.7}$$

where the subscripted numeral 1 is a place holder for the dimensional conversion.

One might regard perfect aggregation as the idealization of typical aggregation in which quantities are affected by changing relative prices. The upshot of the argument here is that the aggregate remains analogous to the macro gas of the ideal gas laws and is not obviously some natural extension of a single underlying molecule. The ideal gas laws fit well only within a limited range of temperatures and pressures. Outside that range, they vary in a manner than can be accounted for using the kinetic theory of gases by adding more realistic assumptions about the volume of individual molecules and the forces acting between them. The equivalent in macroeconomics is found in the efforts of Alan Kirman and Kathryn Dominguez and Ray Fair, among others, to account for distributional effects in macroeconomic relationships.[18]

THE STRANGE CAREER OF THE REPRESENTATIVE-AGENT MODEL

Given what we know about representative-agent models, there is not the slightest reason for us to think that the conditions under which they should work are fulfilled. The claim that representative-agent models provide micro-foundations succeeds only when we steadfastly avoid the fact that representative-agent models are just as aggregative as old-fashioned Keynesian macroeconometric models. They do not solve the problem of aggregation; rather they assume that it can be ignored. While they

---

[18] Kirman (1992), Dominguez and Fair (1991).

appear to use the mathematics of microeconomics, the subjects to which they apply that microeconomics are aggregates that do not belong to any agent. There is no agent who maximizes a utility function that represents the whole economy subject to a budget constraint that takes GDP as its limiting quantity. This is the simulacrum of microeconomics, not the genuine article.

This seems transparently obvious. So why have intelligent economists come to believe so fervently both in the necessity of microfoundations and in the efficacy of the representative-agent model in providing them? Let me offer a speculation. One of the earliest examples of modern dynamic economics is found in Frank Ramsey's optimal savings problem.[19] In this problem, Ramsey considered the problem of saving for an economy and imagined it to be a social planner's problem in which the utility function represented social preferences, without conjecturing how these might be related to the preferences of the members of society. Ramsey may well have thought (in the manner of Keynes) that the wise men of Cambridge could be trusted to know what was best for society independently of any direct knowledge of the lower classes. Push-pin may have been as good as poetry for Jeremy Bentham; but Bentham was an Oxford man. In Cambridge the poets ruled and aspired to rule the world. On Cambridge assumptions, there is no problem with what Ramsey did.

By the early 1950s, the general-equilibrium model had been more thoroughly developed and analyzed. The two theorems of welfare economics were established:

[19] Ramsey (1928).

83

1 Every perfectly competitive general equilibrium is Pareto efficient; and

2 Every Pareto-efficient allocation can be supported as a perfectly competitive equilibrium for some set of lump-sum transfers.

These two theorems appear to promise an isomorphism between social planner problems that choose Pareto-efficient allocations and perfectly competitive equilibria. In fact, this isomorphism provides a powerful technical tool for the solution of dynamic optimization problems, because it is often easier to define a social planner's problem and a Pareto-efficient outcome, and then to ask how to decentralize it, than it is to solve for the competitive equilibrium directly (a trick common in the literature on real-business-cycle models).

Notice that there is a sleight of hand here. Only rarely do macroeconomists care about the redistributions needed to decentralize the social planner's problem. It is fine to ignore redistributions when they do not matter – that is, when all agents are identical and have homothetic utility functions. Once again, the macroeconomists have slipped in unwarranted microeconomic assumptions, as well as, implicitly, assumptions about the shape of the social planner's function. But, if we take the notion of decentralization seriously, we know that everyone cannot be alike. Furthermore, not only does aggregation theory tell us that we do not know how the social planner's function might relate to the underlying utility functions, the older Arrow Impossibility Theorem tells us that, for reasonable assumptions, no social planner's function exists that respectfully and democratically aggregates individual preferences.[20] Thus, the idea of the representative agent appears to arise naturally in dynamic macroeconomic models as a kind of benign extension of Ramsey's social planner in the face of the two welfare theorems. But this idea is plausible only when the macroeconomist fails to take microeconomics seriously.

Could we, nevertheless, not regard the representative-agent model as an idealization? It may be a good way to think about macroeconomic problems when the losses due to aggregation are relatively small. Let us accept that, but notice that whether or not the representative-agent model is a good thing depends now entirely on its contingent empirical success. It may work; it may solve the Lucas critique; it may not. We just have to see. There is no longer a point of principle involved. The advocate of the representative-agent model has no right to attack other macroeconomists for failing to provide microfoundations, for he fails to provide genuine microfoundations himself.

My guess is that the representative-agent model may help in pointing to some sorts of qualitatively useful relationships. But it is unlikely to provide useful quantitative restrictions on the behavior of macroeconomic aggregates. The reason can be seen by thinking about the way in which Marshall used the idea of the representative firm. For Marshall, the representative firm was not the average, or even median, firm, but a firm that typified

[20] Arrow (1951).

85

firms at a point in their life cycle at which the extreme behaviors associated with very small or very young firms, on the one hand, or very large or very old firms, on the other hand, could be set aside. If we can analogize back to the physicist's ideal gas, Marshall wanted to describe the usual behavior of a gas molecule under certain ideal conditions. The use of representative-agent models in modern macroeconomics attempts something quite different. It attempts to describe the behavior of the gas (its pressure and volume), not by considering seriously how the molecules behave in aggregate, but by analyzing the gas as if it were one big molecule subject to the laws that in fact govern real molecules. This is a category mistake: pressure and volume are descriptions of the properties of aggregates – properties that individual molecules either in reality or idealized to colossal size do not possess as isolated units.

On the analogy with gases, we should conclude that what happens to the microeconomy is relevant to the macroeconomy but that macroeconomics has its own descriptive categories and may have its own modes of analysis. It is almost certain that, just as in the case of gases, no genuine microfoundations can ever be provided for macroeconomics that do not make concessions to the macrolevel in the form of statistical assumptions about the distributions of important microeconomic characteristics. And, given those concessions, it is almost certain that macroeconomics cannot be euthanized or eliminated. It shall remain necessary for the serious economist to switch back and forth between microeconomics and a relatively autonomous macroeconomics depending upon the problem in hand.

Does Macroeconomics Need Microfoundations?

SUGGESTED READINGS

As observed in this lecture, the history of microfoundations is a long one. The modern obsession with microfoundations as the sine qua non of macroeconomics can be dated to Robert E. Lucas, Jr.'s "Econometric Policy Evaluation: A Critique" (originally published in Karl Brunner and Allan H. Meltzer [eds.], *The Phillips Curve and Labor Markets*, vol. 1 of Carnegie-Rochester Conference Series on Public Policy, Amsterdam: North-Holland, 1976, and reprinted in Lucas's own *Studies in Business Cycle Theory*, Oxford: Blackwell, 1981). An excellent methodological study of the necessity of microfoundations is found in Maarten Janssen's *Microfoundations: A Critical Inquiry* (London: Routledge, 1993).

More particularly, the modern ploy of providing microfoundations through the representative-agent model is brilliantly attacked in Alan Kirman's "Whom or What Does the Representative Individual Represent?" *Journal of Economic Perspectives* 6(2) (1992), 117–36, and, with a rich historical perspective, in James Hartley's *The Representative Agent in Macroeconomics* (London: Routledge, 1997).

4

Causality in Macroeconomics

In Pissarides's model – in either its theoretical or empirical versions – there are a number of variables, all related to each other through mathematical functions. A natural question is, which of these variables are the causes and which are the effects? (This is not restricted to particular models; the question can also be asked about the economy itself, independently of particular representations of it.) Now, what kind of question is that? To the man in the street – although he may never have thought about economics at all beyond wondering where his paycheck was coming from, how much the government was going to take from it, and how he might spend it – this seems a perfectly straightforward question. The commonsense notion of causation has to do with control or some variant of it: making things happen, recipes, and so forth. That my flipping the switch *causes* the light to come on means that I can use the switch as an instrument to control the light. My placing baking powder into a cake batter causes the cake to rise because baking powder is an instrument for leavening; which is to say that, were I to omit the baking powder, the cake would not rise. We learn causal relationships from babyhood, and they are essential to our making our way in the world. Nothing could be simpler or more straightforward.

But not to economists. Economists long ago ceased to regard the question "does *A* cause *B*?" as straightforward. They tend to identify cause with something different from control. For example, Clive Granger identifies cause with incremental predictability; and Edwin Burmeister, with unique solutions to dynamical systems of equations.[1]

---

[1] Granger (1969) and Burmeister (1980).

Other economists treat causality as if it were a property of models put there by our analytical choices rather than a structural feature of the world.[2] And others, such as Milton Friedman, try to avoid causal talk altogether since it seems to be that one can never get to the bottom of a causal account: the causes have deeper causes, which have deeper causes in turn, and so on.[3] My sympathies are with the man in the street. Although I do not deny that economics presents its own special problems for causal analysis, economists have tended to complicate rather than clarify those problems. It is time to recover common sense. It remains an interesting question, however, how we came to the present impasse.

DAVID HUME AND AFTER

The two most important contributions to our understanding of causality are due to Aristotle and to the Scottish philosopher David Hume. To Aristotle we owe the distinctions among *material cause* (the stuff of which a causal system is constructed), *formal cause* (the organization of that stuff), *efficient cause* (what makes the stuff go from one state to another), and *final cause* (the direction or end to which that movement is tending). Modern analysis has tended to drop off final cause as too anthropomorphic a notion for physical sciences, though it is not obvious that

---

[2] Hendry et al. (1990), p. 184. Hendry's belief is puzzling in the context of his declaration that he is a realist.

[3] Friedman in Hammond (1992), pp. 91–98.

economics, as a social science, should also avoid anthro-
pomorphism. And, in most contexts, material and formal
causes are taken for granted. The real substance of a
theory of causality is found in the analysis of efficient
causes.

Interestingly, both Aristotle and Hume have credentials
as economists as well as philosophers. Indeed, Hume,
despite a very limited number of economic works, remains
one of the great economists of all time. His statement of
the quantity theory of money in an open-economy context
(the so-called specie-flow mechanism), which is found in
his three essays, "Of Money," "Of Interest," and "Of the
Balance of Trade," is classic.[4] In his life, Hume was more
famous as a historian and an essayist. Today, he is remembered more as a philosopher. There has been little attempt
to view Hume as a man of parts with a unified vision. It is
a rare philosopher who bothers to ask whether Hume the
economist has anything to say to Hume the philosopher.
That is too bad, because I think that he does.

Hume's account of causality is a central part of his
epistemology, or theory of knowledge. The key to Hume's
account of knowledge is his radical empiricism. To Hume,
the only things that we know are either immediate sensations or the memories of past sensations. Even abstract
ideas are faded sense impressions. All knowledge is either
empirical (experimental) or mathematical (and he gives an
empirical account of mathematics). So what do we know
when we know a causal relationship? Hume analyzes a
typical case: one billiard ball striking another and causing
it to move. Our knowledge, he says, consists in three things.

[4] Hume (1742a, b, c).

First, the cause is spatially contiguous with the effect (one billiard ball causes another to move when it touches it). Second, the cause precedes the effect (the ball that moves first is the cause; the other is the effect). Third, the cause must be necessarily connected to its effect (the action of the first ball reliably sets the second ball into motion).

The first two elements are easily squared with Hume's epistemology of sense impressions. But where does the idea of necessary connection come from? It is in necessary connection that the commonsense notions of control and of the power or the efficacy of causes find their natural home. But Hume stared at his billiard balls for days, weeks, and months and found in them no source for the idea of necessary connection. Finally, Hume concluded that necessary connection was not to be found in the objects at all; rather, it was to be found in the human mind. But in Hume's epistemology all ideas come from sense impressions, so where does this one come from? Hume finally decided that what the mind feels as necessary connection has its source in the constant conjunction of cause and effect. It is not just that one billiard ball strikes another and then the second ball moves; it is rather that *every* time one strikes, the other moves. Eventually, our minds (without logical warrant, for Hume also attacks the validity of induction) come to regard the effect as the *inevitable* consequence of the cause.

Subsequent philosophers have, I think, often misunderstood Hume. He does not reject the notion of necessary connection; he merely attempts to explain its source. He does not deny that there may be necessary connections in the objects, only that human beings can perceive them directly. Nor does he say that constant conjunction *is* necessary connection, only that this is where our idea of necessary connection arises. Still, many philosophers since Hume concentrate on constant conjunction. Once that is given, philosophical, scientific, and economic accounts of causality differ mainly in where they place the emphasis.

For some, temporal order is the essential thing. The difference between a cause and an effect is that the cause precedes the effect. Of course, we all know the famous fallacy, *post hoc, ergo propter hoc*. I switched on the lights just moments before the ground began to shake with the San Francisco earthquake. That, of course, was startling. But, on reflection, I do not imagine that I *caused* the earthquake.

Others focus on contiguity and constant conjunction. Cause is a shorthand for functional or lawlike relations. If always $A = f(B)$, then some might say that such a relationship is causal. But which is cause and which is effect? If the function is not invertible, then it might seem natural to say that B causes A. But suppose that this relationship is $A = 7B$. Why should we not rewrite it as $B = (1/7)A$? Cause and effect are ambiguous. One possibility is to say that the one that we can directly control is the cause, and the other is the effect. But that begs the question; for what is control other than cause by a different name? Others have tried to solve this dilemma by combining functional order or lawlikeness with temporal order to give an idea of predictability according to law. The function might then be written $A_{t+1} = f(B_t)$; and, even in the invertible case, $A_{t+1} = 7B_t$, rewriting it will not confuse the matter, since causes must precede effects. Later, I will question the usefulness of time order as a causal criterion – at least in economics. But we need to look at some other issues first.

95

Hume's account is deterministic; it is about what always must happen. Of course, economics is not deterministic. Hume anticipates the problem and allows that causal relations may be only probabilistic. His idea of probability is that it is a measure of our ignorance. Deep down, all causal relations are deterministic; but, when we are ignorant of the complete sets of causes, sometimes things happen and sometimes they do not. A probabilistic account of causality replaces constant conjunction with the notion of *robust correlation* and the notion of deterministic laws with *probabilistic laws*.

Having slipped from determinism to indeterminism does not change the nature of the general objections to using mathematical functions or lawlikeness as defining characteristics of causality. In Lecture 2, I questioned the usefulness of the idea of a scientific law for economics. I still question it. But one can easily see the attractiveness of the idea of law or, at least, of a principled account of robustness. We all know that causation does not equal correlation (an idea that is nearly as familiar to the man in the street as it is to the statistician). The appeal to lawlikeness or robustness is meant in part to distinguish causal relations from mere correlations.

What is the problem? The main difficulty with correlation is that it is a symmetrical, but intransitive relationship. If A is correlated with B, then B is correlated with A (this is obvious in the mathematics of the correlation coefficient). If A is correlated with B and B is correlated with C, it nevertheless does not follow that A is correlated with C. (For example, let A and C be independent random numbers and let B be the sum of A and C.) In contrast, the most characteristic feature of a causal relation is that it is asymmetrical and transitive. If A causes B, in general B does not cause A. If A causes B and B causes C, then A causes C. These considerations do not rule out a priori the idea of mutual causation. Rather, they make it a complex relationship consisting of separate causal relations running in opposite directions. The essential thing is that asymmetry and transitivity capture the idea that causal relations are instruments of control or manipulation through which powers are efficaciously transmitted (to use a number of the synonyms for "cause").

The difficulties here are not problems of stochastic formulation; that is, they arise not just because statistics such as correlation are involved in our usual formulations of the issues. They arise even in deterministic contexts. The issue of symmetry already showed up in the difficulty of representing a causal relationship as, for example, $A = 7B$. The equal sign is a symmetrical operator and cannot represent a causal relationship all by itself. Nor can many asymmetrical operators unaided. Consider the logical relationship of implication: $A \rightarrow B$ (read A implies B). In logic it follows that $\sim B \rightarrow \sim A$. But if rain causes the wheat to grow, it is perfectly true that ceteris paribus we can infer logically from the wheat not growing that it has not rained. Nevertheless, we do not believe that by interfering to stop the wheat from growing we can control the rain. Something more than the asymmetry of implication is needed to capture the sense of controllability implicit in our idea of cause. The economist Herbert Simon and the philosopher Nicholas Rescher refer to any formal relationship that fails in this way as having foundered on the "rock of contraposition."[5] No formal relationship that contraposes will in itself capture our sense of causality.

This is where Hume left the philosophical analysis of causality. The next two hundred years of causal analysis is Hume's legacy. On the positive side, he laid out the major issues. A good account of causal relations needs to answer a conceptual question (what does it *mean* to be a cause?), an ontological question (what *are* causes really?), and an epistemological question (how do we *infer* the existence of a casual relationship?). Hume gave his most influential answer to the first question, denied that human beings are capable of answering the second, and gave a detailed analysis of the human practice in using induction to answer the third. He offered an analysis of the third question, despite his famous claim that induction lacks logical warrant.[6] On the negative side, more than anything else, Hume's denial that "necessity" could mean anything more for us than an expectation born of constant conjunction has led to the failure of Hume, and of all his successors as well, to capture what common sense believes about causes.

Hume's famous skepticism is grounded in an unsupportable philosophical idea – namely, that all knowledge comes directly or indirectly from sense impressions. If we deny that idea, then there is no reason for us to deny that we have an understanding of necessary connection that is different from constant conjunction. Oddly, Hume, the his-

---

[5] Simon and Rescher (1966), p. 323.

[6] Hume's argument is that there is no deductive warrant, because any deductive argument would require an inductively established premise to connect it to the world, which would of course beg the question. Similarly, there could be no inductive warrant, as that would directly beg the question.

torian and the economist, takes his skeptical objections far less seriously than does Hume, the philosopher. Switching hats, he writes more in the mode of common sense:

> But still it is of consequence to know the principle whence any phenomenon arises, and to distinguish between a cause and a concomitant effect. Besides that the speculation is curious, it may frequently be of use in the conduct of public affairs. At least, it must be owned, that nothing can be of more use than to improve, by practice, the method of reasoning on these subjects, which of all others are the most important; though they are commonly treated in the loosest and most careless manner.[7]

Writing about international monetary theory, Hume overthrows various popular views with detailed accounts of the "correct" mechanisms, dismissing the mistaken accounts because "a collateral effect is taken for a cause, and . . . a consequence is ascribed to the plenty of money; though it be really owing to a change in the manners and customs of the people."[8]

Hume, the economist, views causality as involving control, the transmission of power or efficacy (notions that he denounced as ungrounded in his philosophical writings), and as structural in the sense that casual relations can be assembled (much as, for Nancy Cartwright, parts with capacities can be assembled) into mechanisms (nomological machines). Eventually, I wish to develop Hume the economist's notion of causality somewhat

---

[7] Hume (1742b), p. 304.   [8] Hume (1742b), p. 294.

further. Now, however, I want to look at the fate of Hume the philosopher's idea of cause, especially as it has come to be used in economics.

PROBABILISTIC CAUSALITY

Modern probabilistic theories of causality begin with the assumption that truly constant (that is, exceptionless) conjunction is too strong a condition to be useful.[9] Rather than constant conjunction, probabilistic accounts look for relationships that tend to hold on average and for the most part. Crudely, A causes B on probabilistic accounts if $P(B|A) > P(B)$, where "$P(X)$" means "the probability of X" and "$X|Y$" means "X conditional on Y." The most prominent causal analysis in macroeconometrics, due to Granger, falls into the class of probabilistic accounts.[10]

Probabilistic causality aims to answer questions such as does taking aspirin cause headaches to end? This might be investigated in a controlled study in which headache sufferers are given aspirin and the results noted. The conjunction will not be constant. But aspirin will be said to cause headaches to end if the probability that one's headache will end if one takes an aspirin is greater than the probability that one's headache will end unconditionally (that is, whether one takes an aspirin or not). Consider an example: suppose that in a trial using 100 patients (50 given aspirin, 50 given a placebo) the results are as reported in Table 4.1.

[9] Suppes (1970) is the classic statement.   [10] Granger (1969, 1980).

100

Causality in Macroeconomics

Table 4.1. *Results of 100 trials*

	Treatment	
	Placebo	Aspirin
Headache does not end	40	20
Headache ends	10	30

On the basis of the data in Table 4.1, we estimate
$P(Headache\ Ending|Taking\ Aspirin) = 30/50 = 3/5 > 40/100 = 2/5 = P(Headache\ Ending)$. So, the probabilistic account implies that taking aspirin causes headaches to end.

The probabilistic theory of causality in its simplest form is faced with a formidable difficulty: $P(B|A) > P(B)$ implies that $P(A|B) > P(A)$; that is, if A causes B, then B causes A.[11] Notice that the data in Table 4.1 show that $P(Taking\ Aspirin|Headache\ Ending) = 30/40 = 3/4 > 1/2 = 50/100 = P(Taking\ Aspirin)$. According to the definition, the headache ending causes patients to take aspirin: but even the advocates of the probabilistic account naturally resist this implication.

This is an example of an important problem in econometric analysis known as *observational equivalence*.[12] The problem does not arise for Hume or anyone else willing to insist that causes must precede effects, because

[11] $P(A\&B) = P(A|B)P(B) = P(B|A)P(A)$, which implies $P(A|B)/P(A) = P(B|A)/P(B)$. Since $P(B|A) > P(B)$, $P(B|A)/P(B) > 1$, which implies $P(A|B)/P(A) > 1$ and, therefore, that $P(A|B) > P(A)$. Q.E.D.

[12] See Simon (1953), Basmann (1965, 1988), and Sargent (1976).

$P(B_{t+1}|A_t) > P(B_{t+1})$ does not imply that $P(A_{t+1}|B_t) > P(A_{t+1})$, where the subscripts are time indices. We rule out the conclusion that the headache ending causes the patient to receive the aspirin, because in no cases does the ending of the headache precede the receiving of the aspirin.

If A precedes B and $P(B_{t+1}|A_t) > P(B_{t+1})$, Patrick Suppes refers to A as a *prima facie cause* of B. A is not a *cause simpliciter*, because there are clear circumstances in which we do not believe that A causes B in which the conditions for prima facie causality are not fulfilled. The classic example is a falling barometer. Although it is a prima facie cause of a storm, we do not generally regard it as a genuine cause of a storm. Economic examples also exist. The money supply rises in late November and early December; it is a prima facie cause of Christmas sales; yet we do not think that the rising money supply genuinely causes Christmas sales.

The idea of a common third cause is illustrated in Figure 4.1. Here later times are indicated above earlier times (t_3 later than t_2 later than t_1) and the arrows show the true causal connections. Hans Reichenbach refers to this characteristic pattern as a *conjunctive fork*.[13] The conjunctive fork is also reflected in a characteristic pattern of conditional probabilities. While in each case in Figure 4.1, $P(B|A) > P(B)$, $P(B|A\&C) = P(B|C) > P(B)$. Conditional on C, A does not raise the probability of B at all; C is said to *screen off A*. A more satisfactory definition of probabilistic cause might then be: A causes B if A is a prima facie cause of B and if there are no intervening C's that screen A off from B.

---

[13] Reichenbach (1956), pp. 158 ff.

Time

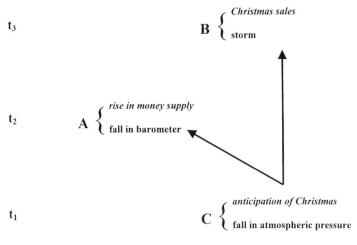

t_3 **B** $\begin{cases} \textit{Christmas sales} \\ \text{storm} \end{cases}$

t_2 **A** $\begin{cases} \textit{rise in money supply} \\ \text{fall in barometer} \end{cases}$

t_1 **C** $\begin{cases} \textit{anticipation of Christmas} \\ \text{fall in atmospheric pressure} \end{cases}$

Figure 4.1.

Reichenbach places the conjunctive fork and the no-screening-off condition in the center of his causal analysis. He adopts an axiom that he calls the *common cause principle*: "If an improbable coincidence has occurred, there must exist a common cause." So, if *A* and *B* are correlated, either *A* causes *B*, or *B* causes *A*, or they have a common third cause, *C*.

The history of the probabilistic approach is one of posing counterexamples in which the probabilities violate our causal intuitions and then of making adjustments to the probabilistic definition of the causal relation that preserve the insight of the original notion of prima facie cause while rendering it adequate to our intuitions. Consider one much analyzed causal puzzle. Birth control pills

103

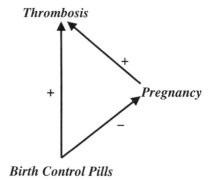

Figure 4.2.

contain chemicals that are known to clot blood, yet the probability of coronary thrombosis (that is, blood clots in the heart) conditional on taking birth control pills is *lower* than the unconditional probability of thrombosis – that is, $P(Thrombosis|Pills) < P(Thrombosis)$ – which suggests that birth control pills do not cause thrombosis but instead reduce or inhibit thrombosis. The puzzle is explained by observing that pregnancy raises the probability of thrombosis and birth control pills lower the probability of pregnancy. The observed probability of thrombosis conditional on taking birth control pills is the net result of a direct and an indirect effect as indicated in Figure 4.2. The plus and minus signs indicate whether the adjacent link indicates a cause that promotes (raises the probability of) or inhibits (lowers the probability of) the effect. Whether $P(Thrombosis|Pills)$ is greater or less than $P(Thrombosis)$ depends on the relative quantitative strength of the three causal linkages.

If Figure 4.2 describes the situation accurately, then the example suggests further restrictions that might be placed on the probabilistic definition of cause. First, the definition might be restricted only to direct causes with a more general *cause simpliciter* defined with relation to the causal ancestors of the effect. But this is not quite enough, for while it clears up the linkages between birth control pills and pregnancy and pregnancy and thrombosis, it leaves the initial puzzle unresolved. Pregnancy is not an intervening third cause in the sense that it will completely screen off the effect of the birth control pills. It is a partial screen. Suppose that we were to divide women in the sample into those who became pregnant and those who did not, then for each of these subgroups $P(Thrombosis|Pills) > P(Thrombosis)$. A second restriction might next be imposed: the definition might require *contextual unanimity*; that is, the change in probability must be the same in all homogeneous backgrounds (for example, whether pregnant or not).

These are just two of many adjustments proposed to resolve puzzles in the probabilistic account of causality. The strategy of incremental adjustments to the probabilistic account suggests its own inadequacy. Not every A such that $P(B|A) > P(B)$ is regarded as a cause of B. Much of the effort in developing probabilistic theories of causality is spent on elucidating the refinements necessary for preventing probabilistic relations like prima facie cause from getting it wrong. In the earlier example, despite the fact that the probabilities indicated that the ending of the headache prima facie caused the taking of the aspirin, the advocate of the probabilistic approach rejects the conclusion. Somehow the probabilities got it wrong. But what does it mean to get it wrong? To ask such a question is to have a strong idea of what it is to be right. Certainly, this is partly a matter of causal intuitions. But it is also clear that there is an implicit notion of causal structure involved in setting the agenda for probabilistic causality.

The puzzles and problematic cases that suggested the various refinements to prima facie cause are set with descriptions of the hypothetically true causal mechanism. Often (as in Figures 4.1 and 4.2) they are clarified using path diagrams in which arrows indicate the direction of causal influence and, sometimes, parameters or plus or minus signs indicate the strength or at least the character of the influence. A probabilistic analysis is judged adequate only when it corresponds to the structure of such mechanisms. The primacy of these mechanisms is implicit in the very notion that a probabilistic account must resolve the various problems and puzzles that the hypothetical causal mechanisms describe.

Probabilistic accounts of causality conflate the concept of cause with the method of inferring cause. They commit what Mario Bunge referred to as "the original sin of empiricism" and Roy Bhaskar as the "epistemic fallacy."[14] The advocates of the probabilistic approach, however, find it nearly impossible to be consistent and constantly refer to implicit causal structures. The central thesis of this lecture is that what is implicit in the strategy of the probabilistic approach ought to be explicitly embraced. *Causal structures are fundamental.* Probabilistic accounts are misrepresented when they are seen as elucidating the concept of causality. In fact, they are useful not for conceptual analysis, but as part of the epistemology of inferring causal structure from observations.

[14] Bunge (1963), p. 45; Bhaskar (1975), p. 171.

Causality in Macroeconomics

But what is a causal structure? Here we have to go back and use Hume the economist to fill in the lacunae left by Hume the philosopher. We simply cannot do without notions like power or efficacy. Useful causal accounts are not about correlations or constant conjunctions but about the way things work. Even Hume the philosopher understands the point.

> A peasant can give no better reason for the stopping of any clock or watch than to say, that commonly it does not go right: But an artizan easily perceives that the same force in the spring or pendulum has always the same influence on the wheels; but fails of its usual effect, perhaps by reason of a grain of dust, which puts a stop to the whole movement.[15]

We require a method of describing the mechanism of the economic clock or watch.

Hume speaks of the sense that causes make things happen as *necessary connection*, yet our notion of causality is not well captured by the logical notion of a necessary condition. Consider the simple example of an explosion caused by a set of conditions: dry air, some gas, a match. The match, for instance, is not a necessary condition of the explosion, since the gas might have been ignited by a spark from a flint and steel or an electrode or some such. Nor is it a sufficient condition, because alone the match can achieve nothing.

[15] Hume (1739), p. 132.

J. L. Mackie has attempted to state more precisely how causes are logically related to their effects.[16] He calls a cause an INUS condition of an effect – that is, an *I*nsufficient member of a set of *N*onredundant and *U*nnecessary *S*ufficient conditions for the effect. The match, gas, and dry air together are sufficient for the explosion. Each is unnecessary since the explosion could have happened through many channels. Each is nonredundant, since all are required for the set to be sufficient (this is the idea that the conditions are "necessary in the circumstances that actually obtain"). And each is insufficient, as no one condition alone could cause the explosion.

Mackie's account is known as a conditional or counterfactual analysis of causality because it uses contrary-to-fact conditionals or counterfactuals to explicate the causal relation. Mackie tries to sketch the structure: if causes, then effects. These are counterfactual because it may be that the antecedent "if" is never fulfilled. The account suits our earlier discussion nicely, because the sense in which causes can be used for control is clear: if I control the antecedents to occur, the causes follow in consequence.

This quick summary of Mackie's analysis slides over many important and subtle issues, but it gives us enough to connect it to economics. Simon has given both formal and philosophical accounts of causality that are, in effect, versions of Mackie's analysis. Let us start with the formal analysis.[17] In the following system of equations:

$$a_{11}x_1 + a_{12}x_2 = a_{10} \tag{4.1}$$

$$a_{22}x_2 = a_{20}, \tag{4.2}$$

[16] Mackie (1980).   [17] Simon (1953) and Simon and Rescher (1966).

where the a_{ij}'s are parameters and the x_j's are variables, x_2 might be said to cause x_1 in the sense that one must know the value of x_2 in order to determine the value of x_1, but not vice versa. The variable x_2 is an INUS condition for x_1, but not vice versa. Simon's idea is that causes can be formally rendered as variables block-recursively ordered ahead of effects. It applies just as well to more complex systems. Consider

$$p_{11}q_1 = p_{10} \tag{4.3}$$

$$p_{21}q_1 + p_{22}q_2 = p_{20} \tag{4.4}$$

$$p_{33}q_3 = p_{30} \tag{4.5}$$

$$p_{42}q_2 + p_{43}q_3 + p_{44}q_4 = p_{40} \tag{4.6}$$

Equation (4.3) is a *minimal self-contained subsystem* of equations (4.3)–(4.6): if one knew the values of the parameters p_{10} and p_{11}, one could determine the value of q_1 in equation (4.3) without reference to any other equation. Equation (4.5) is also a minimal self-contained subsystem. Equations (4.3) and (4.4) together are a *self-contained subsystem*, although not a minimal one: once one knows their parameters, both q_1 and q_2 can be determined. Since the value of q_1 is independent of the value of q_2, whereas the value of q_2 is not independent of the value of q_1, q_1 causes q_2. Equations (4.3)–(4.5) are self-contained. Similarly, equations (4.3)–(4.6) are self-contained: q_1 causes q_2; and q_2 and q_3 cause q_4.

Unfortunately, Simon's account is not adequate as far as I have presented it. It is the old problem of even an asymmetrical formal relation not being adequate unless we can say more about control. Compare equations (4.1) and (4.2) to another system of equations consisting of equation (4.1) and a replacement for (4.2):

$$a_{11}x_1 + a_{12}x_2 = a_{10}, \tag{4.1}$$

$$b_{21}x_1 + b_{22}x_2 = b_{20}. \tag{4.7}$$

Here x_1 and x_2 would appear to exhibit mutual causation or simultaneity. The values of the variables, however, may be the same in each system. This is possible, for example, if either of two sets of identities holds:

$$b_{21} = a_{11}, b_{22} = a_{12} + a_{22} \text{ and } b_{20} = a_{10} + a_{20}, \tag{1}$$

or

$$a_{22} = (a_{11}b_{22}/b_{21}) - a_{12} \text{ and } a_{20} = (a_{11}b_{20}/b_{21}) - a_{10}. \tag{2}$$

This is the problem of *observational equivalence* in another guise.

The solution to the problem of observational equivalence, and the solution to the conundrum of which is the correct causal direction, is that we must privilege one set of parameters – either the a_{2j}'s or the b_{2j}'s must be regarded as fundamental. If the former, then equations (4.1) and (4.2) define the causal order, and x_2 causes x_1. If the latter, then (4.1) and (4.7) define the causal order, and causation is mutual. The parameters define the scope of interventions of control in these systems. If (4.1) and (4.2) define the true causal order and I wish to change x_2, I do so by changing a_{22} or a_{20}. To change x_1, I may change either

a_{10}, a_{11}, or a_{12}, or, indirectly, x_2. The important thing about parameters is that they can be changed independently of one another. If (4.1) and (4.2) define the true causal order, the problem with the system of equations (4.1) and (4.7) can be seen to be that the a's and the b's cannot be altered independently of each other.

These assumptions about the independence of parameters and the idea that they can be controlled seems to presuppose causal knowledge as a part of defining causal direction. Earlier I had rejected this sort of circular definition as question begging. Now, I wish to argue that there is really no choice. Simon's account does not allow us to reduce cause to something else. Rather it allows us on the assumption of some causal knowledge to gain some further causal knowledge. It is like the gears of Hume's watch or Cartwright's capacities. We start with the knowledge that they have a causal function, and the manner in which they are assembled represents causal function that goes beyond that with which we began. The fact of the matter is that there are many causes in the world of which we have no genuine doubt. It does no one any good to pretend that we do doubt them. If I drop my pencil, no one doubts that it will fall. Similarly, to take an economic example, no one doubts that a government or central bank can fix the interest rate on its own short-term bonds through open-market operations. Given that undoubted assumption, people have genuine doubts as to whether that interest rate is a cause of money, or GDP, or the longer-term rate of interest on bonds. Similarly, people doubt whether the long-term interest rate causes money or GDP or whether they cause it.

Simon's idea can be developed – as I do elsewhere – in much greater depth. But we lack the time for that. Let us

111

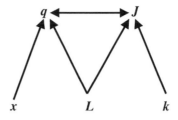

Figure 4.3.

look for a moment at Pissarides's model through Simon's glasses. First, consider Pissarides's theoretical model:

$$J_t = Lk[1 + y + (1 - y)q_{t-1}]q_t, \qquad (1.1)$$

and

$$q_t = \min\{x(J_t/2L, 1), 1\}, \qquad (1.2)$$

Assuming that it is structural, in the sense that its parameters are the privileged ones, he renders the causal relationship between J (jobs) and q (the probability of job match) as one of mutual causation. The other variables, such as L, x, and k, come from outside the system and are rendered as unidirectional causes of J and q. Figure 4.3 shows the causal structure, where the arrows indicate the direction of causal influence.

Interestingly, things are somewhat different with Pissarides's empirical equations.

$$v = F(\phi, w, s, d) \qquad (1.5)$$

and

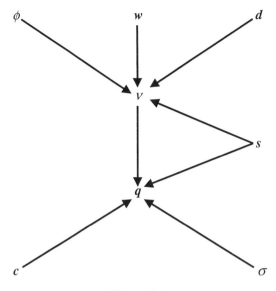

Figure 4.4.

$$q = G(v, s, c, \sigma), \qquad (1.6)$$

Here, v (vacancies) is rendered as a one-way cause of q. The variable s is a common cause; but, like w, ϕ, σ, and c, it is a unidirectional cause. Figure 4.4 shows the causal structure.

These causal relationships are, of course, formal characteristics. An open question remains: to what extent do these formal characteristics correspond to the causal relations that are actually there in the world? I will finish by trying to give an account of how one might shed some light on this question. First, however, I would like to consider the most popular econometric account of causality.

GRANGER-CAUSALITY

When most economists hear the word "causality" they think immediately of Granger-causality – the most influential account of the causal relationship in economics ever. Granger-causality is a variant on the notion of probabilistic cause – one that assumes that temporal ordering is fundamental.

Granger's idea is that A causes B if information about the past of A is incrementally useful in predicting B. So, if

$$P(B_{t+1}|B_t, B_{t-1}, \ldots; A_t, A_{t-1}, \ldots; \Omega_t)$$
$$> P(B_{t+1}|B_t, B_{t-1}, \ldots; \Omega_t),$$

where Ω_t = all information up to time t except for that contained in A and B, then A "causes" B.[18]

Essentially, Granger-causality uses the screening criterion that we discussed earlier. It differs, formally, in the completeness of the information set on which a cause is defined. (Practically, of course, this is nonsense because the implied omniscience is impossible to achieve. More often than not, Granger-causality tests simply ignore Ω_t, making them no different from any other empirical analyses based on conditional probabilities.) It is not subject in theory to some of the paradoxes of probabilistic cause because every possible confounding third cause is embedded in Ω_t. Yet, it still misses important information – for example, in the thrombosis-pregnancy-birth-control-pill case considered earlier, in which there are multiple channels of influ-

---

[18] Granger (1980).

ence. These will be sorted out only if it is plausible to cut the time units very fine. One important objection to Granger-causality in the economic context is that this is not plausible.

In principle, Granger-causality rejects the notion that causes can occur simultaneously with their effects. In fact, Granger admits the case of simultaneous causation (that is, both *A* and *B* enter with the same time index) but regards it as a defect of our economic measurements. I offer two reasons to believe that it is no defect but an irreducible feature of economic analysis. First, consider the relationship between, say, GDP and the general price level. In most countries GDP is measured quarterly (or, at best, monthly) summing up the production of the entire period. Similarly, prices are measured by consumer price indexes or GDP deflators at best monthly – not every price will be measured at the same instant. Granger's argument amounts to saying that what appears to be instantaneous causation will turn out to be temporally ordered if we make finer and finer cuts. Now, when we think what GDP or the general price level is, we can imagine each of them being measured at shorter and shorter intervals. Monthly or weekly GDP makes sense. The idea of instantaneous prices probably makes sense as well. But what about daily or hourly GDP? If we looked at a country, say Holland or the United States, hourly GDP would fluctuate wildly as people came on and off work for meals or at starting and quitting times in most businesses. These fluctuations, I believe, have virtually no causal significance as they do not correspond to any agent's planning horizons. Neither my employer nor I cares that my contribution to output falls every time I take my lunch or step out to the toilet. At some point with GDP, we have made the cut too fine for the economic relations to remain meaningful. There is no guarantee, I think (especially because planning and decision units are heterogeneous and overlapping), that we can eliminate empirically evident instantaneous relationships among economic variables by taking these finer cuts. If the notion of causality is to be useful in economics, it must deal with instantaneous cause.

There is another reason for this as well. Much of our reasoning in economics is about equilibrium states. Equilibrium is a timeless relationship; it occurs when we notionally let time run to infinity so that all the changes in the system are eliminated or allowed to conform to steady-state paths.[19] But just because two variables stand in an equilibrium relationship does not mean that one can be indifferently used to control the other anymore than it means that I can use the height of the barometer to control the pressure of the air. A useful analysis of cause in economics will have to deal with the relationships between equilibrium values of variables without appealing to temporal order.

There is one other difficulty especially pertinent to economics. The situation may be represented in a system of equations as well.

---

[19] The significance of the qualifier "notional" is that equilibrium is, of course, not timeless in that it may be, to use Marshall's categories, market-day, short-run, or long-run equilibrium. The point is that the equilibrium is a state when all the adjustment that is relevant to the problem at hand has been done. The actual temporal process of how it gets to the state is no business of the equilibrium itself.

$$r = a_{10} + a_{11}Y + a_{12}M \qquad \text{LM curve} \qquad (4.8)$$

$$Y = a_{20} + a_{21}r \qquad \text{IS curve} \qquad (4.9)$$

$$M = a_{30} + a_{31}Y \qquad \text{Central bank's} \qquad (4.10)$$
$$\text{reaction function}$$

In this system, r and Y are mutual causes (that is, simultaneous), while M is a unidirectional cause of r. The appearance that r and M are simultaneous is misleading because (4.10) is the central bank's reaction function. What is on the right-hand side of (4.10) is merely what the central bankers choose to react to. In other words, the bank can put any variables it likes on the right-hand side of (4.10) and select the value of the parameters, but it takes the values of the parameters in (4.8) and (4.9) as given by the economy.

Assume that the central bank sets $a_{31} = -a_{11}/a_{12}$. Substituting (4.10) into (4.8) yields

$$r = a_{10} + a_{12}a_{30}. \qquad (4.8')$$

Interest rates are now constant. It would appear that Y no longer causes r, despite the fact that we said that the parameters of (4.8) were given by the economy. (We cannot really do a Granger-causality test on the data in this model since it is deterministic and does not involve lags. But the point generalizes. The apparent incremental correlation between Y and r has vanished. The functional equivalent of Granger-causality has vanished as well.)

Granger-causality is misleading in this case. It is precisely the existence of a structural causal link between money and GDP on the one side and interest rates on the other that keeps the rates constant. In some sense, this is implicit in the presence of a_{30} in (4.8′), as this is a parameter that governs M. But it could be made more perspicuous if we wrote (4.8′) in full as

$$r = a_{10} + a_{11}Y + a_{12}(a_{30} + a_{31}Y) = (a_{10} + a_{12}a_{30}) + (a_{11} + a_{12}a_{31}Y). \qquad (4.8'')$$

Now it is plain that the constancy of interest rates is the result of a *particular* choice of a_{31}, and not a generic characterization of the causal connection. Written this way or any other, however, Granger-causality will fail to correspond to the genuine causal structural that is most efficaciously exploited in this instance.

For physical sciences, philosophers, such as Daniel Hausman, have been willing to dismiss cases that depend on quite particular choices of parameters as being of little interest because those choices of parameters are highly improbable.[20] Unfortunately, that does not work in economics precisely because policy makers are intentional agents, who, unlike molecules, do in fact make choices. This situation is generic with optimal control problems.

INFERENCES ABOUT CAUSAL STRUCTURE

One of the great appeals of causal analysis that depends on conditional probabilities such as Granger-causality is that it appears to be easy to operationalize. If we reject Granger-causality, how should we operationalize causal

[20] Hausman (1998), p. 215.

inference? Let me propose the following scheme, which is worked out in more detail elsewhere.[21] Consider a very simple causal system that corresponds to Pissarides's empirical model of unemployment (U) and vacancies (V):

$$U = a + bV + \varepsilon \qquad (4.11)$$

$$V = c + \omega, \qquad (4.12)$$

where ε and ω are independent random variables. Clearly, on Simon's criterion, V causes U. Now as we noted before, correlation is a symmetrical relation. And so is joint probability. But conditional probability is an asymmetrical relationship. And so are regressions, which can be regarded as a sort of conditional correlation. In fact, if ε and ω are drawn from a normal distribution, regressions are estimates of conditional probability distributions. The asymmetry of the regression is seen in Figure 4.5 which plots the cyclically adjusted values of U against V as in Lecture 2 along with the regressions of U on V and V on U. In some sense, the issue of causal direction is the question of which of these regression lines is correct. Notice that they both have the same $R^2 = 0.68$. They fit the data equally well, so how should we choose between them?

To see why that it is a hard problem, let us consider an artificial model in which V is generated from equation (4.12). The parameter c is set arbitrarily so that $c = 1$, and ω is drawn from a random normal distribution of mean zero and variance one for 100 periods. U is generated from equation (4.11) using the simulated values of V. Its parameters are also set arbitrarily so that $a = 1$, $b = 2$, and ε is

---

[21] Hoover (2001).

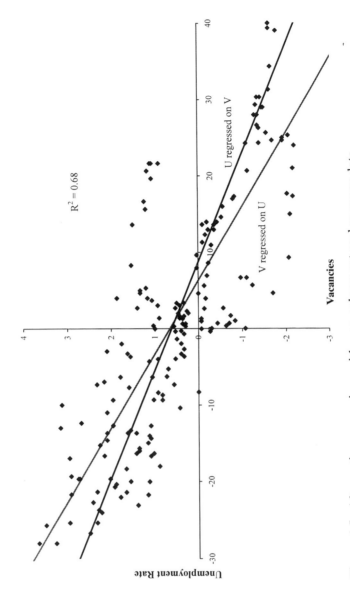

Figure 4.5. Alternative regressions with unemployment and vacancy data.
Source: see Figure 2.3.

120

drawn from a random normal distribution of mean zero and variance one for 100 periods.

We know the true causal ordering, because we constructed the data according to (4.11) and (4.12). In real life, however, we would not know. In ignorance of the true causal order, we might entertain a second possibility. Consider that U could cause V (we ignore mutual causation and causal independence). In that case, the true system might be:

$$V = d + eU + v \qquad (4.13)$$

$$U = f + \zeta. \qquad (4.14)$$

There is no choosing between the systems just from the data alone. Figure 4.6 shows for simulated data the two regressions U on V and V on U that correspond to the two regressions using actual data in Figure 4.1. Again, they are different, since regression is an asymmetrical relationship like causation, but they fit equally well: both have the same $R^2 = 0.87$.

So, is it hopeless? No! Not if we can bring some knowledge from the outside, from history, or from an independent understanding of institutional structure. For suppose, though we do not know the exact form of the process that generates the variables and we do not know to which causal structure it corresponds, that we nevertheless know that there has been some change in the process that governs vacancies, which did not affect unemployment directly. Let us model this by assuming that in period 50, c rose to 5. Figure 4.7 shows a time-series plot of V and the mean before and after the intervention. The break in

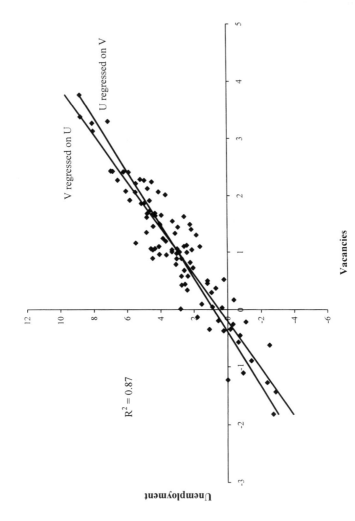

Figure 4.6. Alternative regressions with simulated unemployment and vacancy data.

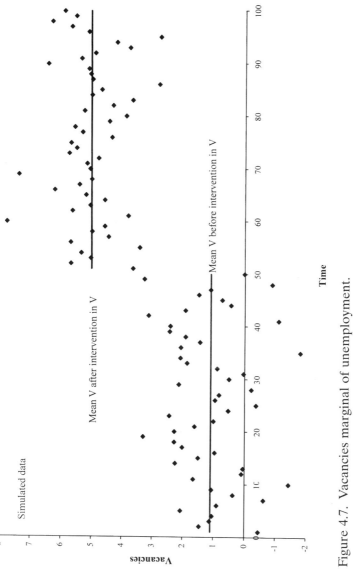

Figure 4.7. Vacancies marginal of unemployment.

the mean is the statistical confirmation of the break that
we know occurred from extrastatistical evidence. How
does this intervention affect other ways of looking at the
data? Figure 4.8 shows the regressions of V on U for the
first and second halves of the sample. The second lines is
clearly shifted up from the first. This means that an intervention in the V process not only affects its mean (V *marginal* of U) but also V *conditional* on U. This is hardly
surprising since the intervention is in the V process. But
consider Figure 4.9. The mean of U is different in the two
halves of the sample; that is, U marginal of V is not stable
in the face of an intervention in V. Figure 4.10 shows that
the regression of U on V hardly changes between the
two halves of the sample (the tiny gap between the two
regression lines is due to sampling variation and is not
statistically significant). In other words, U conditional on
V remains stable in the face of an intervention in the
process that governs V. Ignoring some complications when
forward-looking (for example, rational) expectations are
involved, this pattern is characteristic of a causal structure
in which V causes U: in the face of an intervention in the
causal variable, the probability distribution of the caused
variable conditional on the causal variable remains stable,
and marginal probability distribution of the caused variable displays a structural break.[22]

---

[22] The complication is that rational expectations generate cross-
equation restrictions that make the estimated coefficients of the
conditional regression depend upon the parameters underlying the
marginal regression. The conclusion drawn here does not hold in that
case. Nevertheless, the conclusion of the next paragraph remains
robust even under rational expectations. While this qualification
means that the information of this sort of investigation is less rich as

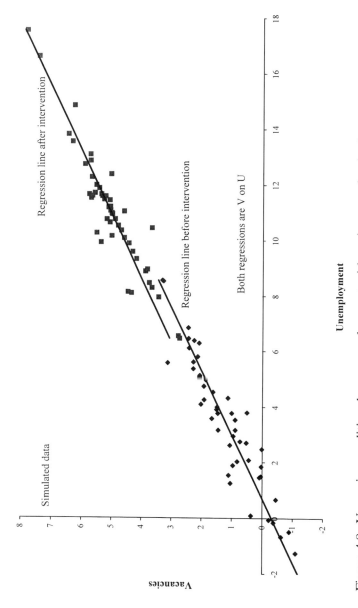

Figure 4.8. Vacancies conditional on unemployment with an intervention in the vacancy process.

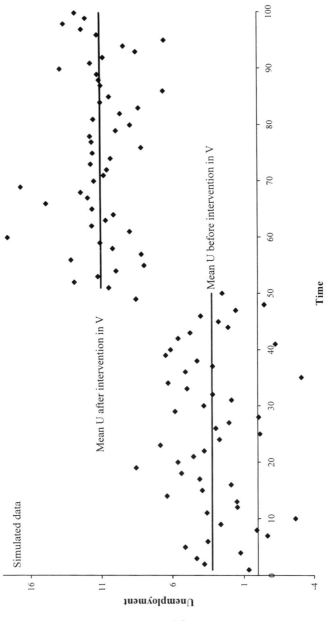

Figure 4.9. Unemployment marginal of vacancies with an intervention in the vacancy process.

126

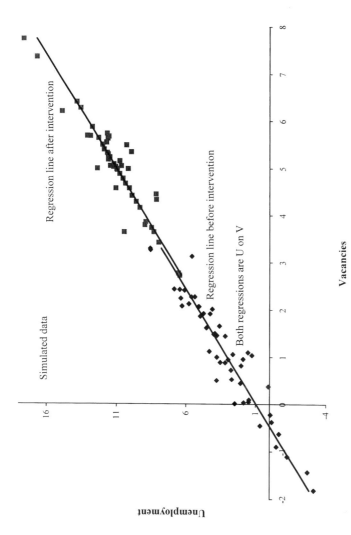

Figure 4.10. Unemployment conditional on vacancies with an intervention in the vacancy process.

127

Now consider another change in structure that we can identify as affecting U but not V independently. We model this by changing b to 4 in equation (4.11). Figure 4.11 shows the mean of U in the two halves of the sample, confirming the intervention. Parallel to the previous case, Figure 4.12 shows that the regressions of U on V in the two halves of the sample are substantially different (in this case a change in slope rather than a change in intercept as in the intervention in the V process). The parallelism breaks down when looked at from other angles. Figure 4.13 shows that the means of V are virtually the same in the two halves of the sample. Again, the small difference between them is sampling variation and not statistically significant. This time, then, it is V marginal of U that remains stable. And Figure 4.14 shows that this time the conditional relationship is not stable: the regressions of U on V for the two halves of the sample are substantially different. This is another pattern characteristic of a causal structure in which V causes U: in the face of an independent intervention in the process governing the caused variable, the marginal probability distribution of the causal variable remains stable, and the probability distribution of the causal variable on the caused variable displays a structural break.[23]

These two patterns are both characteristic of V causing U. Had the data been generated not from equations (4.11)

a source of causal structure than when there are no rational expectations, it usefully provides information as to whether rational expectations are in fact relevant. On these issues, see Hoover (2001), especially Chapters 3 and 7.

[23] The conclusion of this paragraph is, as was noted in n. 22, robust to the presence of cross-equation restrictions owing to rational expectations.

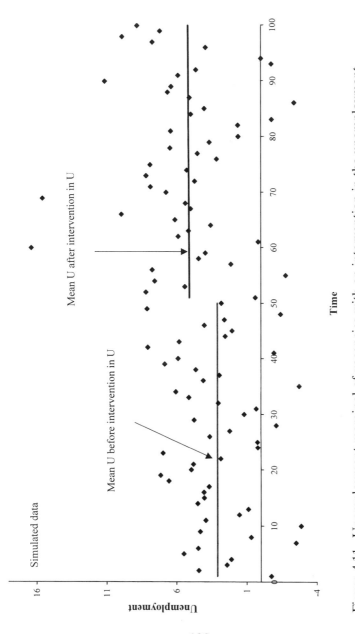

Figure 4.11. Unemployment marginal of vacancies with an intervention in the unemployment process.

129

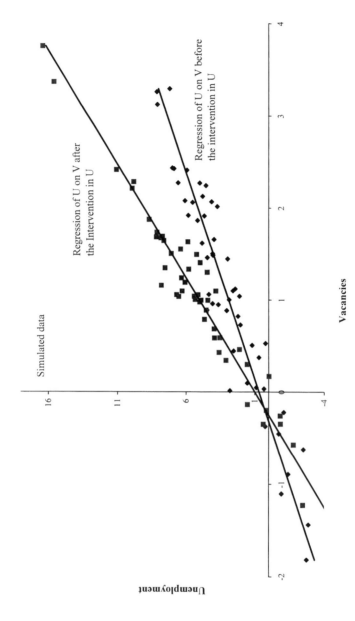

Figure 4.12. Unemployment conditional on vacancies with an intervention in the unemployment process.

130

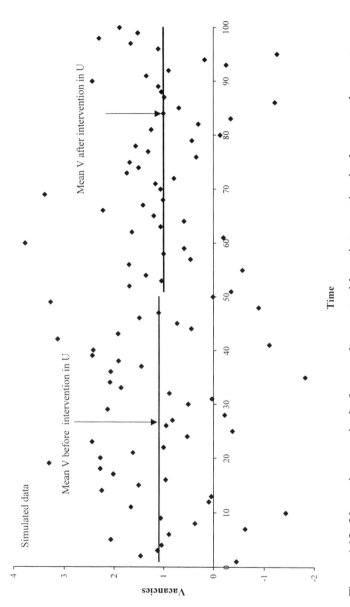

Figure 4.13. Vacancies marginal of unemployment with an intervention in the unemployment process.

131

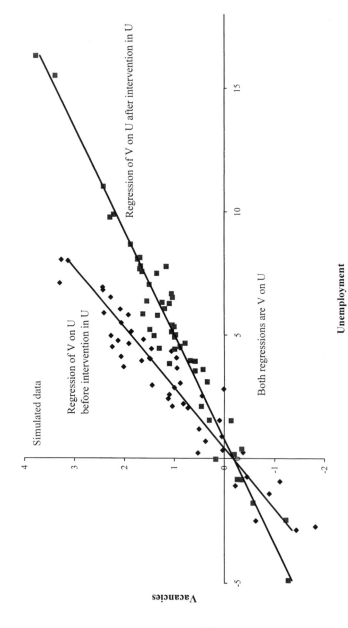

Figure 4.14. Vacancies conditional on unemployment with an intervention in the unemployment process.

and (4.12) but from equations (4.13) and (4.14), these results would have been reversed. The pattern that we have discovered of three equations showing structural breaks while one remains stable is in fact the characteristic pattern of causally ordered systems. If we can identify breaks as belonging to specific parts of the system and if we can discover such patterns, we can identify causal direction.

But that is a big "if." It is the operational equivalent of the previous point that we made: no causes in, no causes out. We need some causal knowledge in order to make further causal judgments. That knowledge cannot come from statistics alone, but requires us to have rich information about the economy. Sometimes that is quite hard. But sometimes it is possible and allows us to say something that we otherwise could not about causal relationships and the possibilities of control in the economy.

SUGGESTED READINGS

My own thinking on causality is explicated much more fully in my *Causality in Macroeconomics* (Cambridge: Cambridge University Press, 2001). These views were developed in a long series of methodological and applied macroeconomic articles. While my book and its antecedent articles have many sources, only a few of the most important ones are mentioned here. The first is Herbert Simon's classic paper of 1953 "Causal Ordering and Identifiability" (reprinted in his *Models of Man*, New York: Wiley, 1957, Ch. 1). Simon provided an account of causality that mapped particularly well into econometric practice. Simon also joined the philosopher Nicholas Rescher in building a bridge to philosophical accounts of causality based on contrary-to-fact conditionals in "Cause and Counterfactual," *Philosophy of Science* 33(4) (1966), 323–40. A classic statement of the counterfactual analysis of causation is J. L. Mackie's *The Cement of the Universe: A Study in Causation*, 2nd ed. (Oxford: Clarendon Press, 1980). Because it is the most common notion of causality in economics, exposing the limitations of Clive Granger-causality has been a central part of my own research agenda for many years. I have grown to have a tremendous respect for Granger's analysis and intentions. They are best explained and the limitations of the notion most clearly set out in Clive Granger's own "Testing for Causality: A Personal Viewpoint," *Journal of Economic Dynamics and Control* 2(4) (1980), 329–52. Finally, a more general philosophical work with a bearing on causality that has greatly influenced my thinking is Nancy Cartwright's *Nature's Capacities and Their Measurement* (Oxford: Clarendon Press, 1989).

5

Pragmatism, Realism, and the Practice of Macroeconomics

Pragmatism, Realism, and Macroeconomics

I shall approach macroeconomic methodology in this lecture from a different angle. The first four lectures were grounded in problems that arise in a concrete case in applied macroeconomics – Pissarides's model of the labor market. The point was to insure that some issues of practical relevance to practicing macroeconomists were addressed. One might think of this as a bottom-up methodology. It corresponds more or less to the vision articulated by Alexander Rosenberg (recall Lecture 1) in which a methodology is related to the particular state of the scientific endeavor and necessarily changes as the state of scientific knowledge itself changes.

The questions we addressed using this approach were: Is it correct to regard theories (or models) as composites of economic laws that govern the behavior of data? Can models be regarded as idealizations? And, if so, how do idealizations connect to reality? What is the relationship between theories (or models) more closely connected to data at the macro level and those that are regarded as somehow more basic at the micro level? What is the nature of the causal structure in those models, and how can real observations be brought to shed light on it?

These questions are genuine ones that arise for macro-economists, whether or not they think of themselves as doing methodology. These questions are natural ones and are thought to have a special status as methodological problems only when people see that they generalize beyond the particular contexts in which they are first noticed. Although the methodological bona fides of these problems are beyond doubt, focusing on them presents a different picture of economic methodology than one would get from reading the excellent introductions to the subject found in Mark Blaug's *The Methodology of Economics*, Bruce Caldwell's *Beyond Positivism*, or Daniel Hausman's *The Inexact and Separate Science of Economics*. So, in this final lecture, I turn to the alternative approach to methodology found in works such as these. This approach corresponds to Blaug's definition of methodology cited in the first lecture: methodology is the branch of economics that considers how economists justify their theories and addresses the general relationship between theoretical concepts and justifiable conclusions.

This is a big area in which many fat books have been written in economics and, more generally, in the philosophy of science. Our tour of the issues shall necessarily be breathless, biased, and superficial.

Two threads run through the approach to methodology in the earlier lectures that have never been spelled out fully. The first is that the approach is realistic. I start with the assumption that that there is an economic reality at a greater level of generality than particular economic facts, and a central issue is to determine how our theories (or models) correspond to it. The second is that the most fruitful approach to these issues is through the consideration of concrete cases of macroeconomic analysis. Thus, while I have been essentially concerned with truth, it is the truth of specific cases that interests me most. What are the truths, for example, asserted by Pissarides's model, and how would one assess them?

Let me make a broad assertion, one that I cannot defend fully here: economists are ambivalent about truth. Edward Leamer in a discussion with his fellow econometricians, Dale Poirier and David Hendry, says bluntly, "I . . . do not think that there is a true *data generating process*. . . . [The distributions of economic data are] characterizations of states of mind."[1] Finn Kydland and Edward Prescott argue that theory must be given primacy over data, since we possess well-founded theories – that is, true theories. They never explain how we come to know that the theories are true. They write: "the model economy which better fits the data is not the one used. Rather, currently established theory dictates which one is used."[2] For this reason, they argue that theoretical models cannot be judged econometrically, even though they may want to use the models' quantitative implications in policy analysis. Kydland and Prescott's idea is that theories are fundamentally true in some dimensions and are quite false in others. As usual, Lucas puts this point of view much more clearly: "insistence on the 'realism' of an economic model subverts its potential usefulness in thinking about reality. Any model that is well enough articulated to give clear answers to the questions we put to it will necessarily be artificial, abstract, patently unreal."[3]

These are extreme cases, yet they reflect pervasive attitudes. Economists argue for truth when it suits their purposes and dismiss its relevance when it gets in the way. And, like Kydland and Prescott, they have strong beliefs that – truth or no truth – economics should be played according to certain rules and that any economics (or even, in Kydland and Prescott's view, data) that violate those rules should be dismissed as wrong or not serious.

---

[1] Leamer in Hendry, Leamer, and Poirier (1990), pp. 188–89.
[2] Kydland and Prescott (1991), p. 174.   [3] Lucas (1980), p. 271.

The Methodology of Empirical Macroeconomics

The goal of this lecture is to situate my own approach to methodology and these dominant attitudes in a broader methodological perspective.

FRIEDMAN, POPPER, AND THE TRADITIONAL PHILOSOPHY OF SCIENCE

Empiricism dominated the traditional philosophy of science. Its central concerns were the relationship between particular empirical evidence and the logical warrant of theoretical generalizations. Traditional microeconomics has had very little to do with empirical justification. The theoretical apparatus of microeconomics is based in folk psychology and introspection. It developed deductively. Microeconomics can be, and usually is, taught without appealing to empirical facts as the warrant for its conclusions. It is, of course, a robust empirical generalization that when prices rise, the quantity demanded falls. But we do not find our faith in the downward-sloping demand curve in the multiplication of examples in which this is true. Instead, it is the axiomatic machinery of consumer theory (or its functional equivalent) that convinces us that demand curves slope down. We all know how to derive the downward-sloping demand curve from utility functions and budget constraints. And we know the usual caveats relating to income effects. Every well-trained economist – at least since the marginal revolution in the nineteenth century – has known how. Empirical evidence was, and is, thought to be relevant to demand. Nevertheless, the point from the earliest days of econometrics to the present was not to gather evidence to support or to "test" the theory of demand; it was to quantify those free parameters (the elasticities) of the demand functions that theory had not pinned down.

Economists finds themselves in an odd situation. On the one hand, they wish to be empiricists – to use data to justify their theories. On the other hand, they believe in their theories more than in their data – even though they do not believe that their theories are descriptively realistic. The economists' most typical evasion of this dilemma was articulated in 1953 in Milton Friedman's essay, "The Methodology of Positive Economics." Friedman argued that the truth or realism of a theory (or model) was not salient; what mattered was the theory's predictive success. Friedman is clearly an empiricist, but he advocates a sort of empiricism that does not put the established apparatus of economics at risk. A model is good not because it is true, but because the world behaves "as if" it were true. (Of course, there is a serious question about why the world should be so tractable if the model were not in fact true in some sense.) Many of Friedman's examples are microeconomic, but I suspect that it is no accident that he is, himself, primarily a monetary economist and macroeconomist; for macroeconomics never had an a priori, axiomatic confidence in its theoretical basis – hence the relentless drive for microfoundations discussed in Lecture 3. The siren song of empiricism enchants the macroeconomist more readily than it does the microeconomist.

Every economist ought to read Friedman's essay. It has been so influential that every student of economics is familiar with the "as-if" justification, even if he cannot recall – if he ever knew – its provenance. Friedman's

141

methodology of "as if" has become the best-used tool in the kit of unreflective rationalizations with which economists support their practices. One way of viewing the claims of Kydland and Prescott and Lucas, cited earlier, is as expressions of the "as-if" attitude. They are that – but not merely that.

I do not wish to attempt to explicate or analyze Friedman's essay here. It is like the Bible: it is a rich, but inconsistent work, open to numerous interpretations. There is a huge interpretive literature. People read various philosophical traditions – logical positivism, instrumentalism, falsificationism, conventionalism, Deweyan pragmatism – into the essay. And Friedman, godlike, has sat mutely by for the past half century, declining to confirm, clarify, or elaborate. The best analyses of the essay that I know of are found in an article by Uskali Mäki and in Abraham Hirsch and Neil De Marchi's book.[4] While I will not assert that Friedman belongs to any particular philosophical school, it is fair to say that he belongs to the same family as the main tradition of the philosophy of science represented, for example, by the work of Carl Hempel, cited in Lecture 2. I take this tradition to be a broad one that includes Karl Popper's falsificationist account, as well as the covering-law account of Hempel and related philosophers. This tradition embraces the notion that the truth about observations bears on the evaluation of theories. There is a variety of accounts of exactly what that bearing is. The tradition is compatible with either the view that theories themselves are true (realism) or the view that theories are only man-made tools (instrumentalism). Either way, one

---

[4] Mäki (1992) and Hirsch and De Marchi (1990).

starts with a commonly determinable truth at the observational level. So, if we consider Pissarides's model again, any account in this mainstream tradition would regard its observational consequences as the critical factor in assessing the merits of the underlying theory, although some accounts would allow that the theory itself might not necessarily be true.

Partly because of the affinities between his work and Friedman's famous essay, and partly because, for a time, he dominated thinking in the philosophy of science, and because economics typically latches onto any radical development in philosophy of science with a mean delay of about two decades, Popper has had considerable currency among economists.[5] Popper's central concern is the *problem of induction*. Induction is the logical form that generalizes from a number of concrete instances to the truth of a universal rule. Since Hume (our old friend, the philosopher/economist), induction has been regarded as a problem because it is not obvious why it should be logically compelling. The deduction, A implies B; B; therefore A, is not valid. Many other things might imply B, so noticing that B obtains does not allow us to deduce that A obtains. Much philosophical ink has been spilt over the past 250 years suggesting justifications for induction that do not fall foul of Hume's objection.

Popper's solution is to embrace Hume and accept that his logic is flawless. Popper notices that, while the argument from the truth of a consequent to the truth of its antecedent is not warranted, the argument from the falsity of a consequent to the falsity of an antecedent is valid: if

[5] See, for instance, Caldwell (1991).

A implies *B*; and not *B*; then not *A*. Popper suggests that science replace inductive arguments with a process of *conjectures and refutations*. Empirical evidence never proves any theory to be true, but may prove it to be false, narrowing the range of admissible explanations. The broader the scope of the theory, the bolder the conjecture, and the more information that a refutation carries. So, for Popper, science is a never-ending process that nonetheless becomes more and more focused over time:

theory → prediction;

if the prediction is observed to be true → test further;

and if the prediction is observed to be false → reject the theory.

Popper's account leaves some issues open. One issue is deeply practical. Many of our theories, especially in economics and social sciences, rely on statistical observations for which the crisp notion of truth or falsity is muddied. Does an outlying observation, for example, contradict the truth of the hypothesized distribution, or is it merely a rare draw from the far tail of the distribution? Another issue is that Popper gives no account of where theories come from or how they are constructed. Related to this, is the issue of just what a theory is. Does any statement or set of statements that generate a prediction constitute a theory? The idea of a theory as a black box that converts inputs into predictions is deeply unsatisfying. Part of the appeal of Cartwright's notion of the nomological machine – and, perhaps the main appeal of microeconomics, even when its predictions are empirically weak – is the emphasis on

articulating the structures that generate predictions. Articulation of mechanisms, seeing how things work, is a large
part of what make scientific explanations compelling.

Popper's account has fallen into disfavor. It is not so
much wrong as offtrack, for it has little to say about articulating mechanism. Kydland and Prescott's and Lucas's
methodological pronouncements underscore the importance of such articulation. At first blush, they look like a
ringing endorsement of the methodology of "as if." But
that is only part of it. Neither Kydland and Prescott nor
Lucas is willing to let just anything count as an acceptable
model – no matter how well it predicts. They claim that
models must possess a particular sort of architecture, compatible with neoclassical microeconomics (or, at least, its
representative-agent version). The interesting questions
are ones that Popper cannot help us to answer: why we
should accept such limiting rules? And why these rules in
particular in the case of macroeconomics?

THE PRACTICE OF SCIENCE

The traditional account of the philosophy of science,
including Popper's account, views science as progressing
constantly toward the truth. This is a caricature – though
common enough among critics of the traditional account.
It is a caricature because it overstates the degree to which
such philosophers as Otto Neurath, Rudolph Carnap,
Hempel, and Popper saw scientific progress as linear and
understates the sophistication and breadth of the intellectual considerations that they thought relevant to scientific

practice. Caricatures work, however, because they highlight some genuine features of their subject. In this case, the caricature correctly picks out the optimistic faith of the traditional view, and, at the same time, it reminds us of features of science for which it finds it hard to account.

The first such feature is the constructive aspect of science. Popper subscribed to Hans Reichenbach's famous distinction between the *context of discovery* and the *context of justification*. His own work, like most of the traditional philosophy of science, is concerned largely with the context of justification: given a theory (model), how is it to be evaluated? As we have already seen, Popper has little to say about the context of discovery. Like others in the traditional approach, he is willing to believe that this is a matter for imagination, psychology, or aesthetics but that little can be said, even from a broadly logical point of view. An account of science that cannot say anything interesting about the construction of its main components – theories or models – does not seem complete.

The traditional view is deficient on a related score as well. Previously, we noted Kydland and Prescott's insistence on a definite, even narrow, set of ground rules for macroeconomic models. Such constraints on theorizing are common in science. The scientific imagination is not free to propose just any explanation – the class of explanations that might be legitimately entertained is restricted and narrowed in some way. The traditional view has no explanation for these constraints.

The most influential contribution to filling these gaps in the traditional account is Thomas Kuhn's *The Structure of Scientific Revolutions* (first published in 1962). Kuhn accounted for the sense that theorizing in science is constrained. He argued that, in any field, a particular *paradigm* limits the range of questions researchers can ask and the type of answers that they can offer. *Normal science* in Kuhn's view is the process of developing, applying, extending, and elaborating the dominant paradigm. Normal science corresponds relatively closely to the vision of the traditional approach to science progressing in a straight line.

The term "paradigm" is borrowed from grammar. It refers to an example or exemplar, say, of the declension of a particular noun or of the conjugation of particular verb that serves as a model to copy mutatis mutandis when declining other nouns or conjugating other verbs. Kuhn was notoriously imprecise in his usage of "paradigm." At least two distinct senses run through his discussion. A paradigm is sometimes exactly what its etymology suggests – a particular model used to guide the development of closely related models. Models such as Hicks's IS/LM model, the Mundell-Fleming model of the balance of payments, Samuelson's overlapping-generations model, Kydland and Prescott's real-business-cycle model, and many others are clearly paradigms in the sense of exemplar.

But Kuhn uses "paradigm" in another sense as well – and this is the one that most disciples and critics have picked up on. A paradigm is the gestalt or worldview of a model or theory – the set of assumptions, definitions, forms, goals, and so forth that make a theory into a theory of this kind rather than some other kind. It is what distinguishes Copernican astronomy from Ptolemaic astronomy, or relativistic physics from Newtonian physics, whatever differences might exist in the details of, say, Newton's own theory and

147

subsequent Newtonian theories. In this sense, one might say that Ricardian economics and neoclassical economics or Keynesian macroeconomics and new classical macro-economics belong to distinct paradigms.

Kuhn's idea of individuated paradigms gives rise to the famous title of his book. As science progresses, normal science develops more or less linearly within a paradigm. As the limits of that paradigm are explored, science discovers anomalies – facts that do not fit, inconsistencies in the theory, and other such problems. When these become severe, the time becomes ripe for a *scientific revolution* that involves the replacement of one paradigm by another.

For Kuhn, the constructive logic to model building and the sense of constraint arise from the particular paradigm. Many of the potential paradigm shifts or revolutions in physical and biological sciences are obvious: Newtonian physics replaced Aristotelian; atomic theories of matter replaced continuous; evolutionary biology replaced non-evolutionary. But the term "scientific revolution" was current before Kuhn – even in economics: witness "the Keynesian revolution" (the title of Lawrence Klein's 1946 book) or the "marginalist revolution." It is one thing to see a revolution in the history of science; it is quite another to conclude that revolutions take Kuhn's particular form of a paradigm shift. Much of the persuasive force of Kuhn's account comes from his linking of his notion of paradigm shift to the preexisting category "scientific revolution." But, in fact, that may be a clever equivocation.

A revolution according to Kuhn is a radical discontinuity. He claims that the concepts of one paradigm cannot be translated into those of another paradigm. The term "mass" may be common to Aristotelian, Newtonian, and relativistic physics: but it bears a different meaning in each; and the different meanings are, in fact, *incommensurable*. Some followers have suggested that each paradigm is like a pair of special glasses through which the world looks completely different (and in extreme versions *is* completely different). To me, the incommensurability thesis appears plausible only when it is described in these vague and metaphorical terms. It seems unable to account for a number of facts. If theories are incommensurable, how is a historian such as Kuhn able to write a history of them all? Similarly, why is it that even relativistic physicists are still trained first in Newtonian mechanics that is barely changed in structure or pedagogy since the seventeenth century? Or, how is it that new classical and Keynesian economists can debate the details of each other's models? Finally, theories from different paradigms appear to have implications for the same measuring instruments. Are they not commensurable at least on these dimensions?

Kuhn's account retains a certain linearity: normal science follows revolution, which in turn is followed by normal science and the prospect of a future revolution. To Imré Lakatos, originally a disciple of Popper, this was an unsatisfactory feature of Kuhn's vision of science. Lakatos proposed an alternative account of science that might be regarded as Popper in light of Kuhn. Rather than a sequence of scientific revolutions, Lakatos proposed that the actual practice of science consists of competing *scientific research programs* in different stages of their life cycles.

Lakatos's scientific research programs are characterized by a set of *hardcore propositions* that are never to be questioned (competing scientific research programs are largely differentiated by their hardcores), and these provide the common elements that are shared by different models in the same scientific research program. The hardcores are surrounded by a protective belt consisting of *positive* and *negative heuristics*. These are guidelines for what to seek and what to avoid in the elaboration and development of the scientific research program. Lakatos's account is motivated by three observations. First, science is not linear; several paradigms appear to coexist in many cases. Second, unfavorable empirical evidence does not cause us to abandon a general approach in the straightforward manner of Popper's falsificationism. Third, even accumulated falsifications or anomalies do not cause scientists to abandon an approach unless there is the prospect of a better approach on offer. Lakatos's account has an evolutionary flavor: different scientific research programs compete for the same scientific niche; they grow, mutate, decline, and, eventually, are superseded by fitter scientific research programs.

Lakatos's account proved to be even more popular among economists than Kuhn's.[6] We can illustrate what is involved in this account with an example of the new classical macroeconomics interpreted as a scientific research program.[7]

The hardcore of the new classical macroeconomics is encapsulated in the following propositions:

[6] Latsis (1976) and De Marchi and Blaug (1991).
[7] The description that follows is quoted from Hoover (1991), pp. 365–66.

HC1 The economy consists fundamentally of self-interested individuals (methodological individualism).

HC2 The economy is characterized by complete interdependence (general equilibrium).

HC3 Real economic decisions depend only on real magnitudes and not on nominal or monetary magnitudes (no money illusion).

HC4 The economy is in continuous equilibrium (that is, every agent successfully optimizes up to the limits of his information).

HC5 Agents' expectations are the same as forecasts generated by the true economic model of the economy (rational expectations).

The negative heuristic of the new classical program could be summed up in the simple injunction, "do not violate any hardcore propositions." The new classicals, however, border on puritanical in their lust for prohibitions; so it is well to be more specific.

NH1 Avoid underived supply and demand curves (no ad hoc models).

NH2 Avoid irrational expectations.

NH3 Avoid partial equilibrium.

NH4 Avoid non-neutrality.

NH5 Avoid disequilibrium.

NH6 Avoid aggregation.

NH7 Avoid unidentified reduced forms.

The characteristic practices of the new classical macroeconomics can be summarized in the positive heuristic, which includes propositions something like the following:

PH1 Construct general equilibrium, dynamic optimization models.

PH2 Use representative-agent models.

PH3 Test over-identifying restrictions.

PH4 Test the ability of models to mimic the variances and covariances of the actual economy.

PH5 Use state-of-the-art mathematical techniques.

The program described here appears plausibly to describe the new classical macroeconomics. But we should be suspicious; for it does not do so uniquely. Other commentators have situated the new classical macroeconomics as part of a broader Walrasian program or even as part of a program that comprises all of neoclassical economics. Furthermore, the positive and negative heuristics described here – and, indeed, in all such programs that I have seen described – are vague and give little serious guidance as to how to proceed in developing the program. Despite the supposed unrevisable status of the hardcore, there are no propositions in it that a new classical economist might not sacrifice under enough provocation, and there are few for which one cannot produce concrete examples of such sacrifices.

My objection to the methodology of scientific research programs is that it fails to individuate research programs uniquely. The reason is that the aspects on which Lakatos focuses do not have normative force for the practitioners. Actual economists do not say – not even implicitly – "this is hardcore," "I must do this," "I cannot do that, if I am to keep with the program." Instead, they look to concrete examples of models that work – and of ones that do not work – and ask how they might alter or adapt them to suit the case to hand. The idea here owes more to Kuhn than to Lakatos – but it is to the Kuhn who takes "paradigm" to mean a concrete exemplar, not to the Kuhn who takes it to mean a gestalt.

There *are* research programs, but they do not follow the strictures of Lakatos's forms. The philosopher Ludwig Wittgenstein denied that a concept, say, "game" or "chair," has a common essence. Rather, he said, all the things that we call games or chairs are collections of overlapping similarities. Two games may have virtually nothing in common, but each may be similar in *different* ways to any number of other games, much the same as two people in the same family may not look much like each other but may, nonetheless, each clearly have the family look. The games might be said to bear a *family resemblance* – and so too the models of a research program.

The appearance of a hardcore and the discipline of the protective belt of positive and negative heuristics arise not from a definite code held by the adherents to a research program, but from the preeminence and success of a particular class of models whose members bear a strong family resemblance to one another. We shall understand more about the new classical macroeconomics through studying the nature of, and reflecting on the potentialities of, Lucas's 1972 incomplete information model of the Phillips curve, or Kydland and Prescott's 1982 real-business-cycle model, or Samuelson's 1958 overlapping-generations model with money than we will by trying to write down or adhere to a set of Lakatosian rules. Seeing research programs as families helps to explain the plausibility of Kuhn's historical account. Some models serve more readily and have greater resonance as exemplars than others.

Working out families of related models – the typical stuff of doctoral dissertations – is Kuhn's normal science. Occasionally, a model of radically different design is offered. It could be thought of as introducing a scientific revolution and creating a new family of normal science. But the family metaphor is an apt one: for we know that no matter how strange, no man or woman is sui generis; we all are cousins at some remove. And so too with models. We may find the manners of our cousins uncouth or the gestalt of a model strange, but they are not *in principle* incomprehensible. The thesis of radical incommensurability is surely false.

ANTIFOUNDATIONALISM

It is common to caricature the traditional philosophy of science, and especially the logical positivism of the 1930s from which it grew, as resting on the claim that all knowledge flows from indisputably secure foundations. There is, of course, an element of truth in this as in other caricatures. Like Hume, who is an essential precursor, the logical positivists thought highly of the evidential merits of sense data. Nevertheless, it is easy to forget that it is to Neurath, a premier logical positivist, that we owe the antifoundationalist metaphor that science is a raft constructed at sea without any firm ground to stand on, or that Popper's

Logic of Scientific Discovery begins with chapters that deny the notion of an a priori sense foundation for science, or that Carnap, another important logical positivist, was an admirer and sponsor of Kuhn's *Structure of Scientific Revolutions* – usually interpreted as an antifoundationalist tract.

The antifoundationalism in Kuhn is related to the thesis of incommensurability. Theories are interpretive and data too are interpreted. In economics this is obvious. A notion such as involuntary unemployment is a theoretically disputed concept, so that whether the statistics collected by the government measure it – or anything – is itself disputable and disputed.

The locus classicus of antifoundationalism predates Kuhn. It is Willard Quine's "Two Dogmas of Empiricism" (first published in 1951). Quine attacks logical positivism as dogmatic. For Quine, logical positivism rests on two propositions: first, analytic propositions are true from logic alone, while synthetic propositions are true only in virtue of empirical facts; and, second, all meaningful statements can be reduced either to logical or empirical facts. Quine argues that these bases for logical positivism lack any principled argument or support. They are the result of giving arbitrary privilege to the claims of the senses and to the rules of logic. (It should be remembered that Quine is one of the great logicians of the twentieth century.)

Quine likens knowledge to a web of mutually supporting, interlocking beliefs on which sense data impinges. When we encounter an observation inconsistent with some of our beliefs, it is not obvious that we need, in the manner of Popper, to reject our belief automatically. For the observation itself and its meaning are also beliefs. We might reject the truth of the observation (it was perhaps a mistake or an illusion) or its import (it can be explained without violating our theory), or we could reject a collateral assumption inessential to our theory, or we could even abandon the principle of logic that makes it inconsistent. Quine argues that, while most of the time we protect some beliefs (such as the rules of logic) from such revision, there is no reason in principle why we should always privilege a particular set of beliefs. If we choose to privilege *any* belief, it is always possible to do so and to maintain it come what may, provided that we are willing to make substantial enough alterations to the other interlocking beliefs in our web.

Quine's argument was anticipated fifty years earlier by the French physicist Pierre Duhem. It is now known as the the *Duhem-Quine* or *Quine-Duhem thesis*.

Quine, of course, recognizes that science would lack its familiar character if some beliefs were not, in fact, privileged. His point is that such privilege is not given in nature, but in human decision. Both Kuhn's paradigms and Lakatos's scientific research programs can be seen as attempts to articulate the conventional basis for such privilege in light of the Quine-Duhem thesis.

AMERICAN PRAGMATISM, RHETORIC AND REALITY

One of the frequently drawn consequences of the Quine-Duhem thesis is that *truth* is a dispensable concept. (I think that this is a mistake – we shall consider why presently.) At a minimum, the Quine-Duhem thesis has led people to believe that truth is not enough, that it must be supplemented with something. But what? Practically, there can be no science unless somehow concrete, particular theories, models, or explanations are chosen. Any replacement for truth still must guide choice. And there would be no point in wanting a replacement for truth unless one were still ready to deny the existence of a privileged position with respect to science.

One school of philosophy that has attempted to integrate the lessons of the Quine-Duhem thesis is recent American pragmatism. Richard Rorty is its most important proponent.[8] Recent pragmatism has its roots in the philosophies of William James and John Dewey. A very crude version of the pragmatic axiom is, whatever works is right. Truth is replaced by some notion of functionality, and that is usually cast in a social context. The issue is not what is true or false, but what promotes our way of life. Rorty stresses the importance of dialogue, conversation, persuasion. He feels justified in doing so, since the Quine-Duhem thesis pushes us toward conventional decisions over what we hold constant and what we have to leave up for grabs. Rorty advocates pragmatism as a tolerant point of view, because it refuses to license anyone to stake out a position that is justified by the unalterable facts of the world.

Rorty's pragmatism is the basis for a sort of intolerant tolerance. We recognize that there are many games and that people, not nature, choose the rules, but if we are

[8] Rorty (1979, 1982).

playing my game and you do not like the rules, I tell you to go home and play your own game.

This implication of Rortyan pragmatism is clear in the work of the literary critic Stanley Fish.[9] Fish is tolerant in that he recognizes many possible interpretive games. Each is determined by the social conventions of a community of interpreters. Some may seem to us to be crazy: his example is an *interpretive community* that takes William Faulkner's gothic tale of the American South, "A Rose for Emily," as a story about Eskimos. All that matters to an interpretive community is the consistency within that community.

Defining communities in this way builds a wall around them. And Fish is a willing mason. There is no point, he argues, in telling the community for whom Faulkner writes about Eskimos that the story is *really* about the South. It is as if someone were to say to an American football player that his touchdown was illegal because he carried the ball to the goal and that is illegal in European football. The proper response is to say, "Get lost! It's a different game that we're playing."

For Fish, this is an appropriate response of any interpretive community to the criticisms of an outsider. Each community can be intolerant of the criticism of outsiders. Unlike sports, interpretive communities do not have formal rules or conventions. Their rules exist only in the tacit assent of the players. Rorty's and Fish's pragmatism thus replaces *epistemic privilege*, the idea that some sort of knowledge (for example, sense data) is privileged, with *social privilege*, the idea that some people are players and that others are outsiders to the game.

---

[9] Fish (1980, 1988).

All this may seem remote from economics, but it is not. The economist and historian of economic thought Roy Weintraub has adopted Quine's outlook indirectly from Rorty and Fish.[10] Weintraub and, similarly, Donald (later Deirdre) McCloskey advocate a pragmatic approach to economics. For Weintraub, economists practicing in a particular field form an interpretive community vis-à-vis noneconomists and economists in other fields. The members of these communities agree on what to privilege, what goals to pursue, what presuppositions to accept, and what conventions to adopt. Thus, Weintraub has argued that it makes no sense for other economists to criticize general-equilibrium theorists for failing to provide a convincing mechanism for price formation or for failing to pass tests of empirical relevance. For these are not related to the goals and values of the general-equilibrium community per se. Another consequence of Weintraub's view is that methodology – the subject of these lectures – cannot matter to economics, as it professes to employ standards external to the interpretive communities its analyzes.

Deirdre McCloskey's *rhetoric of economics project* makes similar claims from a similar starting point. McCloskey attacks *modernism*, which, for her, comprises logical positivism, economic methodology, what I have called the "traditional philosophy of science," and any other recent philosophical trend of which she disapproves. McCloskey argues that we can forget about truth and reality – what we should be concerned about is persuasive argument. Unfortunately, McCloskey never gives a consistent or persuasive analysis of what constitutes good

---

[10] Weintraub (1990, 1991).

argument – that is, argument that we ought to regard as persuasive.

A major consequence of McCloskey's argument is that methodology and philosophy are branded as outsiders to economics and, therefore, as incapable of contributing to conversations *within* economics. This is just like Weintraub – but it is odd that it should come from McCloskey, as she is fond of quoting poets and citing Greek and Latin writers as part of her own rhetoric of economics. And surely, they are outsiders too. Nor does it easily explain why explicitly methodological arguments have *in fact* persuaded economists. For example, Percy Bridgman's operationalism is a major justification for Samuelson's theory of revealed preference. There can be no doubt that Samuelson, the font of the ubiquitous style of modern economics, is an insider to the economics community. Similarly, *economists* routinely justify microfoundational models on the basis of methodological individualism and reductionism and idealized models on the basis of Friedman's "as-if" argument. More than that, it is odd that so many economists have also been philosophers of note (or vice versa): John Locke, David Hume, Adam Smith, John Stuart Mill, Augustin Cournot, Karl Marx, Frank Ramsey, John Maynard Keynes (perhaps), and Amartya Sen, just to give a partial list.

For all that, the rhetoric program has received a relatively warm reception among practicing economists. McCloskey says, quite believably, that few of the skeptics come from among practicing economists. Frank Hahn has recently excoriated methodology as of no practical relevance to economics, and as a waste of economists' time, for reasons similar to McCloskey's.[11] And, indeed, this is an old theme. Irving Fisher used his presidential address to the American Statistical Association in 1932 to attack the critics of method as people who would tell the economist how to get results without having ever gotten results of their own.[12] This, I suspect, gets to the heart of the matter. It is natural and perfectly human not to appreciate or accept criticism from people whom we do not respect and who do not really know what we do. McCloskey's popularity among practicing economists arises mostly because the rhetoric program allows them to regard this natural attitude as perfectly justified and not as narrow-minded or parochial.

THE PRAGMATISM OF C. S. PEIRCE

McCloskey and Weintraub and many economists want economists to concentrate on their particular economic interests. They want outsiders to leave them alone. I agree halfway with this sentiment. Lectures 2, 3, and 4 were meant to illustrate that methodology should focus on the problems that truly matter to economics from a position of genuine knowledge of the subject. But McCloskey and Weintraub and their supporters go off the rails. They draw the wrong lessons from Quine's insight that everything is interpretative. They draw three conclusions from reading Quine: first, nature (or society regarded as nature) imposes

[11] Hahn (1992).   [12] Fisher (1933).

no constraints; anything goes within the interpretive community, as long as one remains socially acceptable. Second, communication between different communities is (and should be) limited: the incommensurablity thesis. And, third, truth is a dispensable notion for progress within disciplines.

The older pragmatism of the greatest American philosopher, C. S. Peirce, I think evades these unhappy conclusions, without losing their insights.[13] For Peirce, what matters is belief. When we believe, we are (temporarily at least) satisfied. Belief is interpretive. Just as for Quine, even perceptions are beliefs, and therefore interpretive, which preserves the antifoundational insight. Beliefs are always relative to doubts. A belief settles a doubt. A real doubt inhibits our actions; a real belief is one that we act on. People sometimes profess to doubt something, but do not really doubt it, as they continue to act on it. There are many ways to fix our beliefs and to assuage our doubts. Scientific inquiry is one way (and for Peirce the best way, though we cannot give his full argument here).

We cannot start off doubting everything or we could never act, even to pursue an inquiry. We do not start with the truth. We start with those things that we truly do not doubt and aim our inquiry at those things that we truly do doubt. It is belief rather than truth that is normative, because the world does not come with labels "this is true," "that is false."

One of the things that we do not doubt is the reality of general relationships. The sign of that reality is the relationships' resistance to being ignored. We believe certain

---

[13] Hoover (1994).

general things about the world, for example, that walls are really solid, because if one tries to walk through them, one feels a resistance, and one cannot practically bring oneself to ignore it. Similarly, there is an old joke that if you torture data long enough it will confess; but empirical economists know that this glib quip is false. Data are recalcitrant; it is hard to make them say what one wants them to say. In contrast, Weintraub rejects realism. He claims that all the general claims of a theory are just patterns that we impose, like the patterns of the constellations that we impose on the stars. It is easier for Weintraub to believe this because he is a theorist, not an empirical economist who has felt the recalcitrance of data.

Truth is important even though belief is regulative. Truth, in Peirce's view, is a fully adequate description of reality (something we do not have and therefore, *at best*, is an ideal at which we aim). A procedure for fixing belief is ultimately going to be successful only if it respects the truth about reality. Of course, we do not ever know that we have finally obtained the truth. So, on the one hand, Peirce advocates *fallibilism*: nothing we believe is ever perfectly secure from the possible need for revision. At the same time, he maintains that there are some things we believe so surely that it would be silly not to act as if they are *indubitable*.

Fallibilism supports Quine's idea that anything might be revised in the face of a recalcitrant experience. But notice that we need the indubitability of some beliefs as well. Quine says we are *forced* to revise our beliefs, but where does the sense of force or inconsistency come from? Quine's metaphor of the web works only when some beliefs are held fixed, because the indubitable beliefs

define which is the web, which are the experiences imping-
ing on the web, and when the two are in conflict. Many
years ago, I saw a device on which one spins a child's top
and it keeps spinning for days. Only those who believe that
perpetual motion machines are impossible – many people,
of course, have no views on them whatsoever – find the toy
to be interesting, because only that belief tells us that
something is fishy and that we ought to be trying to discover the trick.

Notice that Peirce's notion of truth and realism promotes tolerance. If, like Weintraub, I maintain that things
are whatever I decide they are, then there is no reason at
all why I should consider your view of the matter. But
if I say there is a Truth about Reality, it applies equally to
you and to me. If I recognize that even if I have the truth,
there is no label to tell me that this is so, I then have a
reason to consider your views and to test them against
the world and against my views. Because all of our beliefs
are fallible, you might have discovered something that I
did not.

Peirce's theory of belief gives him a different approach
to the problem of induction. He distinguishes induction
from abduction. Abduction reasons: C; and if A implies C,
then C would follow as a matter of course; therefore possibly C. Abduction sees a fact and then offers a hypothesis, which induction might then test. Abduction seems to
be a weak form of inference in this purely formal account.
Still, if the abduction is surrounded by enough indubitable beliefs of the right kind, abduction might be streng-
thened to be nearly a deduction: the "possibly" turned into
"almost certainly." Most of Sherlock Holmes's so-called

famous deductions are really on this view abductions – hypotheses, but hypotheses that are strongly constrained by some indubitably held beliefs.[14]

This is an extremely superficial account of Peirce, which could not begin to convince you of why he is regarded as so profound. I hope, nonetheless, that it makes clear the sense in which my own philosophy and the point of view of these lectures is *pragmatic* in Peirce's sense of the word.

SUGGESTED READINGS

Relatively unsullied by explicit philosophical concerns, Milton Friedman's "The Methodology of Positive Economics" (in *Essays in Positive Economics*, Chicago: Chicago University Press, 1953) has dominated discussions of methodology among economists for nearly fifty years. It is required reading for anyone who wants to understand the methodological attitudes of economists.

The essential background to the recent debates in the philosophy of science are the basic works of: Karl Popper, represented by his *Logic of Scientific Discovery* (London: Hutchison, 1959; originally published in 1935 German); Thomas Kuhn, with his *Structure of Scientific Revolutions* (2nd ed., Chicago: University of Chicago Press, 1970 [originally published in 1962]); and Imré Lakatos, represented

---

[14] The idea of abduction is related to the idea of bootstrapping (see Hausman 1992), not to be confused with bootstrapping in econometrics.

165

by his "Falsification and the Methodology of Scientific Research Programmes" (in Lakatos and Alan Musgrave, eds., *Criticism and the Growth of Knowledge*, Cambridge: Cambridge University Press, 1970, pp. 91–188). Their contributions are well summarized by a philosopher in William Newton-Smith's *The Rationality of Science* (London: Routledge, 1981) and by economists in Mark Blaug's *The Methodology of Economics: Or How Economists Explain* (2nd ed., Cambridge: Cambridge University Press, 1992) and in Roger Backhouse's *Truth and Progress in Economic Knowledge* (Aldershot: Elgar, 1997). My own reservations about Lakatos are amplified in my essay "Scientific Research Program or Tribe? A Joint Appraisal of Lakatos and the New Classical Macroeconomics" (in Neil De Marchi and Mark Blaug eds., *Appraising Economic Theories: Studies in the Methodology of Research Programs*, Aldershot: Elgar, 1991, pp. 364–94).

The roots of neopragmatism are found in various readings of Dewey by, for example, Richard Rorty in *Philosophy and the Mirror of Nature* (Princeton: Princeton University Press, 1979). Neopragmatism is linked to mainline philosophy of science in part through its appreciation of the arguments of Willard Quine in his famous critical essay "Two Dogmas of Empiricism" (in *From a Logical Point of View*, 2nd ed., Cambridge, MA: Harvard University Press, 1961, pp. 20–46.). Closely allied to Rorty within economics are the antimethodological views of E. Roy Weintraub, well expressed in his "Methodology Doesn't Matter, But History of Thought Might" (in Seppo Honkapohja, ed., *The State of Macroeconomics*, Oxford: Blackwell, 1990, pp. 263–79), and the rhetoric program initiated by Donald McCloskey with an essay that later became the core of *The Rhetoric of Economics* (Madison: University of Wisconsin Press, 1985).

Recent neopragmatism must be distinguished from the original pragmatism of Charles Peirce, which is very different in its animating spirit, though it remains connected to the latter-day versions through the mediation of William James and John Dewey. Peirce is a difficult writer to approach for the first time, because his views are not systematically presented in any compact work. The student should probably begin with his essay "The Fixation of Belief," which is reprinted in many places including in volume 5 of his *Collected Papers* (vols. 1–8, Arthur W. Burks, Charles Hartshorne and Paul Weiss, eds., Cambridge, MA: Belknap Press, 1931–58). Several selections of Peirce's writings have also been published: *Chance, Love, and Logic* (with a supplementary essay by John Dewey. Morris R. Cohen, ed. London: Kegan Paul, Trench, Trubner; and New York: Harcourt, Brace, 1923); *Philosophical Writings of Peirce* (Justus Buchler, ed., New York: Dover Publications, 1955); *Selected Writings (Values in a Universe of Chance)* (Philip P. Wiener, ed., New York: Dover Publications, 1966); and *Charles S. Peirce: The Essential Writings* (Edward C. Moore, ed., New York: Harper and Row, 1972). My own essay, "Pragmatism, Pragmaticism and Economic Method" (in Roger Backhouse, ed., *New Directions in Economic Methodology*. London: Routledge, 1994, pp. 286–315), is meant not only to provide an accessible explication of Peirce's philosophy for an audience of economists but also to present, more fully than in this lecture, a Peircian case against neopragmatism in economics.

Bibliography

Anand, Sudhir, and S. M. Ravi Kanbur. (1995). "Public Policy and Basic Needs Provision: Intervention and Achievement in Sri Lanka." In Jean Drèze, Amartya Sen, and Athar Hussain (eds.), *The Political Economy of Hunger*. Oxford: Clarendon Press, pp. 298–331.

Arrow, Kenneth J. (1951). *Social Choice and Individual Values*. New York: Wiley.

Barro, Robert, and Herschel I. Grossman. (1971). "A General Disequilibrium Model of Income and Employment." *American Economic Review* 61(1), 82–93.

Basmann, R. L. (1965). "A Note on the Statistical Testability of 'Explicit Causal Chains' Against the Class of 'Interdependent' Models." *Journal of the American Statistical Association* 60(312), 1080–93.

Basmann, R. L. (1988). "Causality Tests and Observationally Equivalent Representations of Econometric Models." *Journal of Econometrics* 39 (Annals), 69–101.

Baumol, William J. (1952). "The Transactions Demand for Cash: An Inventory Theoretic Approach." *Quarterly Journal of Economics* 66(4), 545–56.

Begg, David K. H. (1982). *The Rational Expectations Revolution in Macroeconomics: Theories and Evidence*. Deddington, Oxford: Philip Allan.

Bibliography

Bhaskar, Roy. (1975). *A Realist Theory of Science*. Leeds: Leeds Books.

Blaug, Mark. (1992). *The Methodology of Economics: Or How Economists Explain*, 2nd ed. Cambridge: Cambridge University Press.

Bunge, Mario. (1963). *The Place of the Causal Principle in Modern Science*. Cleveland: Meridian Books.

Burmeister, Edwin. (1980). *Capital Theory and Dynamics*. Cambridge: Cambridge University Press.

Cagan, Phillip. (1956). "The Monetary Dynamics of Hyperinflation." In Milton Friedman (ed.), *Studies in the Quantity Theory of Money*. Chicago: Chicago University Press, pp. 25–117.

Caldwell, Bruce J. (1991). "Clarifying Popper." *Journal of Economic Literature* 29(1), 1–33.

Caldwell, Bruce. (1994). *Beyond Postitivism: Economic Methodology in the Twentieth Century*, rev. ed. London: Routledge.

Cartwright, Nancy. (1989). *Nature's Capacities and Their Measurement*. Oxford: Clarendon Press.

Cartwright, Nancy. (1994). "Fundamentalism vs. the Patchwork of Laws." *Proceedings of the Aristotelian Society*, 94, 279–92.

Clower, Robert W. (1965). "The Keynesian Counter-revolution: A Theoretical Appraisal." Reprinted in Donald A. Walker (ed.), *Money and Markets: Essays by Robert W. Clower*. Cambridge: Cambridge University Press, 1984, pp. 34–58.

Cools, Kees, Bert Hamminga, and Theo A. F. Kuipers. (1994). "Truth Approximation by Concretization in Capital Structure Theory." In Bert Hamminga and Neil B. De Marchi (eds.), *Idealization VI: Idealization in Economics*, Poznan Studies in the Philosophy of Science, no. 38, pp. 205–28.

De Marchi, Neil, and Mark Blaug (eds.). (1991). *Appraising Economic Theories: Studies in the Methodology of Research Programs*. Aldershot, U.K., and Brookfield, VT: Elgar.

Dominguez, Kathryn M., and Ray C. Fair. (1991). "Effects of the Changing U.S. Age Distribution on Macroeconomic Equations." *American Economic Review* 81(5), 1276–94.

Bibliography

Dusenberry, James. (1949). *Income, Saving and the Theory of Consumer Behavior*. Cambridge, MA: Cambridge University Press.

Feynman, Richard P. (1985). *QED: The Strange Theory of Light and Matler*. Princeton: Princeton University Press.

Fish, Stanley. (1980). *Is There a Text in This Class? The Authority of Interpretive Communities*. Cambridge, Cambridge University Press.

Fish, Stanley. (1988). "Economics in the Human Conversation: Comments from Outside Economics." In Arjo Klamer, Donald N. McCloskey, and Robert M. Solow (eds.), *The Consequences of Economic Rhetoric*. Cambridge: Cambridge University Press, pp. 21–30.

Fisher, I. (1933). "Statistics in the Service of Economics." *Journal of the American Statistical Association* 28(181), 1–13.

Fitoussi, J. P. and K. Velupillai. (1993). "Macroeconomic Perspectives," in H. Barkai, S. Fischer, and N. Liviatan (eds.), *Monetary Theory and Thought*. London: Macmillan.

Friedman, Milton. (1953). "The Methodology of Positive Economics." In *Essays in Positive Economics*. Chicago: University of Chicago Press, pp. 3–43.

Friedman, Milton. (1957). *A Theory of the Consumption Function*. Princeton: Princeton University Press.

Granger, C. W. J. (1969). "Investigating Causal Relations by Econometric Models and Cross-Spectral Methods." Reprinted in Robert E. Lucas, Jr., and Thomas J. Sargent (eds.), *Rational Expectations and Econometric Practice*. London: George Allen and Unwin, 1981, pp. 371–86.

Granger, C. W. J. (1980). "Testing for Causality: A Personal Viewpoint." *Journal of Economic Dynamics and Control* 2(4), 329–52.

Hahn, F. (1992). "Reflections." *Royal Economic Society Newletter*, no. 77, April.

Hammond J. Daniel. (1992). "An Interview with Milton Friedman on Methodology." In W. J. Samuels (ed.), *Research in the History of Economic Thought and Methodology*, vol. 10. Greenwich, CT: JAI Press, pp. 91–118.

171

Bibliography

Hansen, Lars Peter, and Thomas J. Sargent. (1980). "Formulating and Estimating Dynamic Linear Rational Expectations Models." *Journal of Economic Dynamics and Control* 2(1), 7–46.

Hartley, James E. (1996). "Retrospectives: The Origins of the Representative Agent." *Journal of Economic Perspectives* 10(2), 169–77.

Hartley, James E. (1997). *The Representative Agent in Macroeconomics*. London: Routledge.

Hartley, James E., Kevin D. Hoover, and Kevin D. Salyer. (1997). "The Limits of Business Cycle Research: Assessing the Real Business Cycle Model." *Oxford Review of Economic Policy* 13(3), 34–54.

Hartley, James E., Kevin D. Hoover, and Kevin D. Salyer (eds.). (1998). *Real Business Cycles: A Reader*. London: Routledge.

Hausman, D. M. (1992). *The Inexact and Separate Science of Economics*. Cambridge: Cambridge University Press.

Hausman, Daniel M. (1998). *Causal Asymmetries*. Cambridge: Cambridge University Press.

Hendry, David F., Edward E. Leamer, and Dale J. Poirier. (1990). "The ET Dialogue: A Conversation on Econometric Methodology." *Econometric Theory* 6(2), 171–261.

Hendry, David F., and Mary S. Morgan (eds). (1995). *The Foundations of Econometric Analysis*. Cambridge: Cambridge University Press.

Hicks, John R. (1946). *Value and Capital*, 2nd ed. Oxford: Clarendon Press.

Hirsch, Abraham, and Neil De Marchi. (1990). *Milton Friedman: Economics in Theory and Practice*. New York: Harvester Wheatsheaf.

Hoover, Kevin D. (1991). "Scientific Research Program or Tribe? A Joint Appraisal of Lakatos and the New Classical Macroeconomics." In Neil de Marchi, and Mark Blaug (eds.), *Appraising Economic Theories: Studies in the Methodology of Research Programs*. Aldershot, U.K., and Brookfield, VT: Elgar, pp. 364–94.

Bibliography

Hoover, Kevin, D. (1994). "Pragmatism, Pragmaticism and Economic Method." In Roger Backhouse (ed.), *New Directions in Economic Methodology*. London: Routledge, pp. 286–315.

Hoover, Kevin D. (1995). "Why Does Methodology Matter to Economics? A Review Article." *Economic Journal* 105(430), 715–34.

Hoover, Kevin D. (2001). *Causality in Macroeconomics*. Cambridge: Cambridge University Press.

Hume, David. (1739). *A Treatise of Human Nature*. Edited by L. A. Selby-Bigge. Oxford: Clarendon Press, 1888.

Hume, David. (1742). (a) "Of Money," (b) "Of Interest," (c) "Of the Balance of Trade." In *Essays: Moral, Political, and Literary*. Edited by Eugene F. Miller. Indianapolis: Liberty Classics, 1885.

Hume, David. (1777). *An Enquiry Concerning Human Understanding*. Edited by L. A. Selby-Bigge, *Enquiries Concerning Human Understanding and Concerning the Principles of Morals*, 2nd ed. Oxford: Clarendon Press, 1902.

Jorgenson, Dale. (1963). "Capital Theory and Investment Behavior." *American Economic Review* 53(2), 247–59.

Kirman, A. P. (1992). "Whom or What Does the Representative Individual Represent?" *Journal of Economic Perspectives* 6(2), 117–36.

Klein, Judy L. (1997). *Statistical Visions in Time: A History of Time Series Analysis, 1662–1938*. Cambridge: Cambridge University Press.

Klein, Lawrence R. (1947). *The Keynesian Revolution*. New York: Macmillan.

Kuhn, Thomas S. (1970). *The Structure of Scientific Revolutions*, 2nd ed. Chicago: University of Chicago Press.

Kydland, Finn E., and Edward C. Prescott. (1982). "Time to Build and Aggregate Fluctuations." *Econometrica* 50(6), 1345–69.

Kydland, Finn E., and Edward C. Prescott. (1991). "The Econometrics of the General Equilibrium Approach to Business Cycles." *Scandanavian Journal of Economics* 93(2), 161–78.

Latsis, Spiro (ed.). (1976). *Method and Appraisal in Economics*. Cambridge: Cambridge University Press.

Bibliography

Leontief, Wassily. (1936). "The Fundamental Assumption of Mr. Keynes's Monetary Theory of Unemployment." *Quarterly Journal of Economics* 51(1), 192–97.

Lucas, Robert E., Jr. (1972). "Expectations and the Neutrality of Money." *Journal of Economic Theory* 4(2), 103–24.

Lucas, Robert E., Jr. (1976). "Econometric Policy Evaluation: A Critique." In Karl Brunner and Allan H. Meltzer (eds.), *The Phillips Curve and Labor Markets*. Carnegie-Rochester Conference Series on Public Policy, vol. 1, Spring. Amsterdam: North-Holland, pp. 19–46.

Lucas, Robert E., Jr. (1977). "Understanding Business Cycles." In Robert E. Lucas, Jr., *Studies in Business-Cycle Theory*. Oxford: Blackwell, pp. 215–39.

Lucas, Robert E., Jr. (1980). "Methods and Problems in Business Cycle Theory." *Journal of Money, Credit and Banking* 12(4, part 2), 696–715. Reprinted in Robert E. Lucas, Jr., *Studies in Business-Cycle Theory*. Oxford: Blackwell, 1981, pp. 271–96.

Lucas, Robert E., Jr. (1987). *Models of Business Cycles*. Oxford: Blackwell.

Mackie, John L. (1980). *The Cement of the Universe: A Study in Causation*, 2nd ed. Oxford: Clarendon Press.

Mäki, Uskali. (1992). "Friedman and Realism." In Warren J. Samuels and Jeff Biddle (eds.), *Research in the History of Economic Thought and Methodology*, vol. 10. Greenwich: JAI Press, pp. 171–95.

Mäki, Uskali. (1996). "Scientific Realism and Some Peculiarities of Economics." In R. S. Cohen, R. Hilpinen, and Qiu Renzong (eds.), *Realism and Anti-Realism in the Philosopy of Science*. Dordrecht: Kluwer, pp. 427–47.

Marshall, A. (1920). *Principles of Economics: An Introductory Volume*, 8th ed. London: Macmillan.

McCloskey, Donald N. (1985). *The Rhetoric of Economics*. Madison: University of Wisconsin Press.

Bibliography

Mill, J. S. (1848/1911). *Principles of Political Economy with Some Applications to Social Philosophy*. London: Longman's and Green.

Mill, John Stuart. (1851). *A System of Logic, Ratiocinative and Deductive: Being a Connected View of the Principles of Evidence and the Methods of Scientific Investigation*, 3rd ed. London: John W. Parker.

Modigliani, Franco, and R. Brumberg (1954). "Utility Analysis and the Consumption Function: An Interpretation of Cross-section Data." In K. Kurihara (ed.), *Post-Keynesian Economics*. New Brunswick, NJ: Rutgers University Press.

Morgan, Mary S. (1990). *The History of Econometric Ideas*. Cambridge: Cambridge University Press.

Nowak, L. (1980). *The Structure of Idealization: Towards a Systematic Interpretation of the Marxian Idea of Science*. Dordrecht: Reidel.

Patinkin, Don. (1965). *Money, Interest, and Prices*. 2nd ed. New York: Harper and Row.

Pissarides, Christopher A. (1992). "Loss of Skill during Unemployment and the Persistence of Employment Shocks." *Quarterly Journal of Economics* 107(4), 1371–91.

Popper, Karl. (1959). *The Logic of Scientific Discovery*. London: Hutchison.

Quine, Willard V. O. (1951). "Two Dogmas of Empiricism." In *From a Logical Point of View*, 2nd ed. Cambridge, MA: Harvard University Press, 1961.

Ramsey, Frank P. (1928). "A Mathematical Theory of Saving." *Economic Journal* 38(152), 543–59.

Reichenbach, Hans. (1956). *The Direction of Time*. Berkeley and Los Angeles: University of California Press.

Resnick, Robert, and David Halliday. (1960). *Physics for Students of Science and Engineering*. New York: Wiley.

Robbins, L. (1935). *An Essay on the Nature and Significance of Economic Science*. London: Macmillan.

Rorty, Richard. (1979). *Philosophy and the Mirror of Nature*. Princeton: Princeton University Press.

Rorty, Richard. (1982). *The Consequences of Pragmatism* (*Essays: 1972–1980*). Minneapolis: University of Minnesota Press.

Rosenberg, Alexander. (1992). *Economics: Mathematical Politics or Science of Diminishing Returns*? Chicago and London: Chicago University Press.

Sargent, Thomas J. (1976). "The Observational Equivalence of Natural and Unnatural Rate Theories of Macroeconomics," *Journal of Political Economy* 84(3), 631–40." Reprinted in Robert E. Lucas, Jr., and Thomas J. Sargent (eds.), *Rational Expectations and Econometric Practice*. London: George Allen and Unwin, 1981.

Simon, Herbert A. (1953). "Causal Ordering and Identifiability." In Herbert A. Simon, *Models of Man*. New York: Wiley, 1957, Ch. 1.

Simon, Herbert, and Nicholas Rescher. (1966). "Causes and Counterfactuals," *Philosophy of Science* 33(4), 323–40.

Sims, C. (1972). "Money, Income and Causality." Reprinted in Robert E. Lucas, Jr., and Thomas J. Sargent (eds.), *Rational Expectations and Econometric Practice*. London: George Allen and Unwin, 1981, pp. 387–403.

Suppes, Patrick. (1970). "A Probabilistic Theory of Causality." *Acta Philosophica Fennica*, Fasc. XXIV.

Tobin, James. (1956). "The Interest Elasticity of the Transactions Demand for Cash." *Review of Economics and Statistics* 38(3), 241–47.

Tobin, James. (1958). "Liquidity Preference as Behaviour Towards Risk." *Review of Economic Studies* 25(2), 65–86.

Vercelli, Alessandro. (1991). *Methodological Foundations of Macroeconomics: Keynes and Lucas*. Cambridge: Cambridge University Press.

Viner, Jacob. (1936). "Mr. Keynes on the Causes of Unemployment." *Quarterly Journal of Economics* 51(1), 147–67.

Bibliography

Weintraub, E. Roy. (1990). "Methodology Doesn't Matter, But History of Thought Might." In Seppo Honkapohja (ed.), *The State of Macroeconomics*. Oxford: Blackwell, pp. 263–79.

Weintraub, E. Roy. (1991). *Stabilizing Dynamics: Constructing Economic Knowledge*. Cambridge: Cambridge University Press.

Index

179

Index

Caldwell, Bruce, 138
capacities
  of inductance-capacitance
    oscillator, 30, 32–3
  of mass-and-spring harmonic
    oscillator, 30–1, 33
  of nomological machines, 29
Carnap, Rudolph, 145, 155
Cartwright, Nancy, 7, 28–9, 33, 36,
    37, 41–2, 48, 54, 59, 144
causal direction
  defining, 111
  identifying, 119–33
causality
  Aristotle's theory of, 92–3
  common cause principle
    (Reichenbach), 103
  commonsense notion of, 91, 94,
    98–9
  conditional or counterfactual
    analysis, 108
  conjunctive fork in, 102–3
  contributions to understanding
    of, 92–100
  dealing with instantaneous
    cause, 116
  economists' view of, 91–2
  Granger-causality, 114
  Hume's account of, 92–6
  idea of constant conjunction
    in, 94–6
  of macroeconomic model, 15
  probabilistic, 96, 100–106
  Simon's analysis, 108–10
causal relationships
  asymmetry in, 97
  conjunctive fork pattern, 102–3
  good account of, 98
  Granger-causality account of,
    114

Hume's legacy, 98–100
  as instruments of control, 97
  in Pissarides's model, 112–
    13
causal structure
  inferences about, 118–33
  in macroeconomic model, 15
  in Pissarides's model, 113
  probabilistic accounts to infer,
    106
causation
  distinct from correlation, 96
  in economics, 116–17
  instantaneous, 115–16
  simultaneous, 116–17
ceteris paribus conditions, 27–9,
    36
Clower, Robert, 65
community, interpretive
  of economists in particular
    fields, 159
  of Fish, 158
composite commodity theorem
    (Hicks), 76–9
continuity thesis, 6
Cools, Kees, 36
correlation
  distinct from causation, 96
  symmetrical and intransitive,
    96–7, 119
Cournot, Antoine-Augustin, 62,
    70
Cournot problem, 70, 72, 73–4

data, empirical
  in analysis of causal structure,
    119–33
  gap between idealized models
    and, 39
  to justify theory, 141

180

Index

idealization
  of relationship between model
    and world, 35–7
  of representative-agent model,
    85
  see also models, idealized
individual
  actions in economics of, 60–3
  behavior in Pissarides's model,
    12–13
  grounding macroeconomics in,
    65–8
individualism
  in English and American
    economics, 62–3
  of late nineteenth century, 62
  methodological, 62, 72
  ontological, 72–3
  transition to idea of, 60–2
induction
  defined, 143
  distinct from abduction
    (Peirce), 164
  Hume's objection to, 143
intuition
  causal, 106
  economic, 51

James, William, 157
Jevons, William Stanley, 62
Jorgenson, Dale, 64

Kanbur, S. M. Ravi, 41–2, 52
Keynes, John Maynard, 63–4
King, Gregory, 61
Kirman, Alan, 82
Klein, Lawrence, 64, 148
knowledge
  in causal direction, 111, 119–
    33

epistemic and social privilege
  in, 158
as web of beliefs (Quine),
  155–6, 163–4
see also causal knowledge
Kuhn, Thomas, 146–50, 153–6
Kydland, Finn, 38, 40, 139, 145,
  146, 153

Lakatos, Imré, 149–50, 152, 156
laws
  in civil society, 53
  covering-law model of
    explanation, 20–2
  in economics, 25–9, 53–4
  hierarchical relationship of,
    22–3
  law of demand, 25
  nomological machines that
    make, 28–33
laws of physics
  in capacities of harmonic
    oscillator, 30
  exceptions and conditions in,
    27–8
Leamer, Edward, 138–9
Leontief, Vassily, 64
Lucas, Robert, 40, 59, 65, 71–2,
  139, 145, 153

McCloskey, Deirdre (Donald),
  159–61
Mackie, J. L., 108
macroeconomic models
  as blueprints for nomological
    machines, 33–5, 39–42
  empirical generalizations in,
    26
  ground rules for, 146
  microfoundational, 12–13

182

nomological machines (*cont.*)
  laws as output of, 29
  macroeconomic models as
    blueprints for, 39–42
Nowak, Leszek, 35, 36, 37

observation
  as belief (Quine), 156
  in econometrics, 52–3
  statistical, 144
observational equivalence
  in econometric analysis, 101–2
  solution to problem of
    (Simon's analysis), 110–11
Okun's law, 71
overlapping-generations model
  aggregation in, 14
  infinite number of agents in,
    14
  Pissarides's model as, 8–9

paradigm
  examples of models as, 147
  Kuhn's use of term, 147–8, 153,
    156
  in Lakatos's account of
    science, 150
  meaning of, 147
Pareto efficiency, 83–4
Patinkin, Don, 64
Peirce, C. S., 162–5
Petty, William, 61
philosophy of science
  empiricism in traditional,
    140
  from logical positivism, 154
  Popper's role in, 143, 145–6
  science in traditional account
    of, 145–6
Pissarides, Christopher, 7–16, 19,

26, 34, 38, 40, 41, 42–3, 48,
  59, 91, 112, 119, 137, 143
political economy
  contemporary, 62–3
  of seventeenth and
    eighteeenth centuries, 60–1
Popper, Karl, 142–5, 150, 154–5
positivism, logical
  of Neurath and Carnap, 154–5
  Quine's attack on, 155
pragmatism
  of James and Dewey, 157
  of Peirce, 162–5
  of Rorty and Fish, 157–8
Prescott, Edward, 38, 40, 139,
  145, 146, 153
probability
  asymmetrical relationship of
    conditional, 119
  in causal structure inference,
    106
  conjunctive fork in
    conditional, 102–3
  symmetrical relationship of
    joint, 119
proposition as a law, 20–1

quantity theory of money
    (Hume), 93
Quesnay, François, 61
Quine, Willard, 155–6, 161–3
Quine-Duhem thesis
  in American pragmatism, 157
  truth as dispensable concept
    in, 156–7

Ramsey, Frank, 83, 85
Rapping, Leonard, 65
real-business-cycle models
  to explain macroeconomic

Index